red bird against the snow

restoration of a modern landmark

D1265275

red bird against the snow

restoration of a modern landmark

Dorri Steinhoff

Copyright © 2021, Dorri Steinhoff
All rights reserved. This book or any portion thereof may not be reproduced or used
in any manner whatsoever without the express written permission of the publisher
except for the use of brief quotations in a book review.

First Edition 2021
ISBN: 978-1-950843-46-6

Parafine Press
5322 Fleet Avenue
Cleveland, Ohio 44105
www.parafinepress.com
Cover design by Joe Kuspan
Book design by Meredith Pangrace

"The thing most lacking in the functional house is the quality of a dream; that quality of the environment so necessary to integration."

—Tony Smith

TABLE OF CONTENTS

PREFACE

There is something inherently beautiful when the forces of nature reclaim an abandoned building. What once stood as a testament to human presence is soon overtaken as the elements of wind, rain, and the fluctuations in temperature cause decay over time, reducing the structure to a former shadow of itself. Tall weeds encroach. Vines creep through the cracks as plant life begins to envelope the building. Shards of broken glass, missing from windowpanes, create sharp-edged geometry. A patina forms over the surfaces, casting a nostalgic shadow. People have long traveled to see the ruins of past civilizations while dismissing those they may pass everyday as blight. Neglected and forgotten, many are lost forever as few of us ever take the risk of reviving those fragments of history abandoned.

The Gunning House, known to the family who lived there as Glenbrow, was one of those ruins. Last occupied in 2006, the 1940 organic modernist house and 1964 tower were left uninhabited with virtually no maintenance. Trespassing, vandalism, and insect and water damage had caused such severe deterioration that, although appreciated for its design, interested parties all backed away from committing to its restoration. At the time we discovered it in 2013, exposure to the elements had diminished its deemed value to the point that the property was being sold only for the land.

CHAPTER 1:
Foundation

L ife seems to follow a slow steady path and we sometimes lose ourselves in the banality of our daily routines, but other times, a jolt causes a sharp departure from the course. So it happened on a warm September afternoon in 2013, in bright sunshine on a mundane trip out east of the city to a hardware store while we were restoring a house we had just purchased. That change would take several years and dramatically alter our lives. This is the tale of that journey.

My husband Joe is an architect, devoted to his profession, and I am an architecture aficionado. As part of the University of Notre Dame's architecture program, Joe spent a year studying in Rome—a time that greatly influenced his life as he absorbed classical art and architecture, the spatial quality of Italian cities, and the rich Italian culture. After graduating from Notre Dame's five-year architecture program, he moved to Chicago's Lincoln Park neighborhood—surrounding him was a city known for its architectural treasures. As an intern with the noted architecture firm Skidmore, Owings, and Merrill, Joe reported to the famed architect Walter Netsch—even housesitting at his modernist Old Town home. He was in awe of Netsch's expansive art collection, which included sonambient sculptures by Harry Bertoia, work by Roy Lichtenstein, and several Robert Indiana serigraphs. Netsch assigned him the role of assistant to Isamu Noguchi as he worked on his 1976 fountain, *In Celebration of the 200th Anniversary of the Founding of the Republic,* that faces Grant Park in front of the School of the Art Institute in Chicago. Joe also worked with artist John David Mooney on public art, including Mooney's entry for a competition in Canberra, Australia, and a searchlight installation that was executed on the Chicago lakefront in 1977.

Unlike many architects who work from within the confines of a well-designed office building, Joe enjoys the process of getting his hands dirty and actually building some of what he has created. Lacking in funds but not creativity, he designed and built his furniture, even learning to sew in order to fabricate cushions for his modern sofa. This was the start of much more to come.

Besides his creativity, Joe also possesses what I consider some rare talents, including the ability to visualize in three dimensions and to be able to tune out the world around him. "Draw me a picture, or better yet, how about a 3-D model?" I would insist, frustrated at not understanding what he was imagining in his mind but attempting to describe it in words. I am unable to conceptualize ideas into images. I need sketches. Lots of them.

Our two children, Maren and Sofia, would refer to his other gift as "La La Land," whenever Joe removed himself from the present in order to fully immerse himself in his design process. It was tempting to use his mental absence to get him to agree to requests he normally would not. "Dad, can we get a new puppy?" He would often answer in the affirmative without listening to what was said. Frustrating as it may be to others, these were gifts of his I envied.

I had grown up in the milquetoast outer suburbs of Chicago that were built in the late 1950s and were lacking in inspiration and devoid of character. My childhood respite was an undeveloped field, several hundred acres in size, directly behind our house that served as an immense play area. Part prairie and part dried, exposed clay substrate, it was eroded with deep fissures that captivated the neighborhood children and led to hours of exploring. A creek traversed from east to west through a terrain that gradually descended downhill. At the eastern edge of this field was the community pool—the focus of summer fun—a bare bones facility without heated water that was a far cry from today's aquatic megastructures.

Growing up in the sixties was a time of unlocked doors, playing outdoors until dark, and unstructured activities.

It was stays at my aunt's home in the North Shore enclave of Wilmette that convinced me at a young age that I yearned for more. Her grand old houses had so much character, and the nearby St. Joseph's Catholic Church was awe-inspiring to a young child. I enjoyed walks to the neighborhood soda fountain at the corner drugstore, past dress shops with their imaginative window displays. There was a richer life beyond the banal automobile suburbs of the 1950s and '60s.

In college, I learned to appreciate architecture while studying in Chicago. Tours of Frank Lloyd Wright homes, as well as classes in historic Lincoln Park and downtown Chicago led me to appreciate the vernacular buildings of this great midwestern city. Although most of my classes were at the Lincoln Park campus, I also had classes in a 1916 building, designed by the firm of the famed architect Daniel Burnham, that required rides in gilded elevators with uniformed manual operators who would shut the metal gate, then crank the elevator into motion. Surrounded by impressive buildings, I learned to appreciate their detail and craftsmanship.

After graduating from college, I accepted a job in Woodstock, Illinois—the county seat of rural McHenry County—which was the second-to-last stop on the Chicago Northwestern commuter lines and was the town immortalized in the comedy classic *Groundhog Day*. The quaint midwestern city is known for its charming historic town square that features an 1889 opera house and a county courthouse and jail that have been converted into a restaurant and bar. Having maintained much of the original elements, you could eat in a jail cell once occupied by famed labor organizer Eugene Debs.

I lived alone outside of Woodstock near the town of Greenwood—population about 200 in the early 1980s. Up the road, behind the Greenwood Cemetery, was an old farmhouse owned by a friend's family. The spacious, four-bedroom, white-clapboard-clad house had beautiful wood craftsmanship and was furnished in period antiques. The property featured an old white hay barn and had numerous outbuildings surrounded by several hundred acres of rolling fields that were leased out to a local farmer for cattle grazing. Remnants of an old stone foundation had been converted into changing rooms for a tennis court with the walls extending to surround a built-in pool. There was a more modern aluminum-clad stable with horse stalls and a riding arena. After growing up in a small suburban ranch house shared with six siblings, living in this pastoral setting was nirvana!

As much as I loved living alone in the bucolic setting, long winters could be lonely. The picturesque rolling hills that were so beautiful most of the year became brutal in the windswept winters of northern Illinois. I would leave my car down by the road when drifting snow blocked the passage up the quarter-mile drive and trudge through thick drifts past the old cemetery's weathered headstones in my stylish moon boots. After a couple years, I headed off to graduate school in Cincinnati to begin the next chapter of my life.

Joe and I met at the opulent Netherland Plaza Hotel in Cincinnati while I was in graduate school. The firm Joe worked for was hosting a hospitality suite at the grand 1931 French Art Deco hotel within the iconic Carew Tower. A classmate of mine who was the brother of a colleague of Joe's, thought we had similar interests in music and architecture. "Whether it works out or not, there is free food and drinks and a way better atmosphere than the Dana Inn!" Wayne joked, referring to our usual dive bar hangout.

Joe was restoring an early-1900s two-family foursquare just north of downtown Columbus, Ohio. The summer after we first met, I helped him with a project he was working on—the replacement of 160 feet of sidewalk along his house in Italian Village, a historic working-class neighborhood. He discovered a brick walkway buried beneath years of overgrown turf that extended from a crumbling concrete sidewalk in front of the house. Throughout the summer, we sledgehammered, removed the broken pieces of concrete, excavated the old brick from beneath the weeds, and took inventory of that which was salvageable. "You're my strong Russian woman," Joe would joke in his poorly executed Boris Badenov accent. We hammered away that summer with the beat of the city around us. Afterward, Joe designed a paving scheme using the old bricks and featuring a border of contrasting new brick to form a rectangular pattern that transversed his property along Kerr Street in Italian Village. That summer I played assistant was the first of many projects that we worked on together over the years.

I was working in Cincinnati after graduate school and the distance between us was taxing on the relationship. Unable to find a position in my field in Columbus, we decided to combine my passion for clothing with Joe's talents in architectural design. I had a friend, Tony, who owned a small boutique near the University of Cincinnati. In return for Joe designing a new store for him, he introduced us to the world of boutique retail.

We lived one block east of High Street, the main north-south route that connected downtown Columbus with the Ohio State University campus. This stretch of High Street was known as the Short North. Joe had purchased his small brick house in 1981 for $31,000 at a time when the neighborhood was in a rough state. Rents in the area were cheap, with many of the distressed old buildings being occupied by young artists and others working in creative fields. The business district, once a strip of urban blight, was an up-and-coming, though still fledgling, art district. By the mid-1980s, many boarded-up storefronts were becoming fresh new business start-ups. A visionary real estate developer, Sandy Wood, had recently transformed one of the blighted buildings into a building known as the Carriage House, with storefronts below and restored apartments above. One of the premier restaurants in town, Rigsby's Cuisine Volatile, as well as several art galleries, had recently opened there. The once Old Time Religion Hall, with its fire and brimstone sermons that could be heard out on the street, soon became a thriving jazz club. This was the 1980s, a time when urban renewal and revitalization was seen as positive change that brought people and business back into the downtowns of cities.

The area businesses had recently begun a monthly Gallery Hop, and on the first Saturday of every month, crowds would line the sidewalks, more often to people-watch than to frequent the businesses. At the time, there were two clothing shops: Puttin' on the Dog, which was a vintage clothier with a bright pink neon sign and the front portion of a pink Cadillac in the front window, and Anthony's, a high-end men's shop. In 1987, we decided to open a contemporary young designer boutique, Moda Veritè, between the two existing shops and adjacent to Kenny's Pawn Shop, a holdover from the past. Joe designed and built our shop using ad hoc hardware pieces, steel cable, corrugated metal, and steel pipes from a hardware store. Columns were fabricated from PVC pipes and floor drains. Sconces were made from sawn-in-half galvanized buckets. His inexpensive, creative design won awards and was published in an interior design magazine. I focused on buying and visual merchandising, working the business end of the retail shop.

We enjoyed informal entertaining. Joe owned a workhorse electric pasta machine, which coupled nicely with our passion for cooking. Our door was always open to neighborhood friends, so often an array of creative people would stop by to listen to music and stay for dinner. During one of our many informal dinners in our Italian Village home, Joe collaborated with our friend Chris Steele on the design concept for the Mona Lisa wall mural just down the alley from our house. Chris was the founder of Citizens for a Better Skyline, a not-for-profit group devoted to historical preservation and city beautification through advocating for public art murals. Joe designed T-shirts to raise the money for the mural, painted by Brian Clemons in 1990 on the back of Reality Theatre, a professional experimental theatre engaged in work by the local LGBT community. The theatre was housed in a one-story building that was much longer than it was high, so the painting was irrelevantly positioned sideways so that Mona appeared to be laying on her back. "It's positioned the way it fit," the duo would respond when questioned about the symbolism behind the Italian icon.

Over the course of the next seventeen years, I ran the business while Joe worked his way up the ladder to become Director of Design at a 100-person architecture firm located downtown. We converted the two-family house into a single-family over time, living in the house during renovation. During one particularly long winter, we were living in one side while the only functioning bathroom was on the other side of a brick wall that ran down the middle of the house. This meant descending a steep staircase that would never meet today's code, going outside and around the front of the house to the entrance on the far side, then ascending another set to steep stairs to use the bathroom. If Joe had the audacity to relieve himself in the alley to avoid the distance to the bathroom, I would flash the outdoor lights and yell, "Woo-Hoo!" out the door. "What's good for the goose is good for the gander," I would remind him. When the time came to break through the wall dividing the two sides, we took turns sledgehammering through the brick to form an opening. I was given the honor to be the first to crawl through the crude hole in order to use the facilities.

The double, each side with two compact bedrooms and one bathroom, was transformed into a single-family house with two larger bedrooms and two larger bathrooms. Our main bedroom featured a circular walk-in closet, surrounding a mass that concealed air vents that extended up two stories to an open attic space—reminiscent of one of the towers in San Gimignano, Italy, that we had visited on our honeymoon. "This closet is larger than my Manhattan apartment," exclaimed the performance artist Reno during a visit to our house.

Joe had collaborated with a wood sculptor, Ralph Williams, on the design of two new staircases, the first in oak leading to our bedroom with a circumvolve in which no two steps were identical. Ralph created a sculptural newel post in which the geometry of segments in a spiraling column related to the steps he created for the stairwell. It was the start of a close friendship and many years of working together on various projects.

The second stairwell, which led from our bedroom up to the open attic space, was made from steel pieces Ralph had found at a local metal scrapyard. The handrail was made of alternating layers of thin wood and steel strips that were clamped under so much tension during construction that Joe and Ralph needed to use extra caution during installation. "If these clamps fail, this steel rail will spring like a sharp blade, slicing whatever it comes in contact with," Ralph warned. The two soon bolted all the pieces and the once discarded steel became a piece of sculpture leading to the attic. Joe had opened up the once soot-filled attic, lining the pyramid-shaped underside of the roof with new support beams, which were then covered in drywall. Operable skylights faced the downtown, providing a view of the skyline as well as a warm glow of sunlight from the south. The floor plan played off the 12 1/4-degree true north-south shift of the street grid of Columbus to create knee walls, painted a spring green, that undulated around the room, symbolizing the hills of Tuscany against the two-story, San Gimignano-inspired orange tower that extended from the closet. The ceiling was painted the palest of twilight colors, giving the room an ethereal feeling.

While the hustle and bustle of city life is exciting for young people, my memories spent living alone on a 270-acre farm stayed with me. As much as I enjoyed the energy of the Short North, I missed that solitude of living close to nature that I had during those earlier years. With our Italian Village house now completed, we decided to purchase a weekend home in the country, limiting our search to places within an hour from home. We discovered house project number two just outside of Gambier, the small town that features Kenyon College, a picturesque liberal arts school that had a well-known bookstore open 365 days a year! "Country living with access to the Sunday *New York Times*," Joe would joke. The campus was the backdrop for the 2012 film *Liberal Arts*, written and directed by Josh Radnor.

After the flat landscape of Columbus, the rolling hills with old farmsteads and the quaint white clapboard churches of Knox County were a welcome change. We came across our weekend property on a warm spring day when the trees were just beginning to bud. The densely wooded, ten-acre site had a long winding driveway that led to an A-frame house and a three-and- a-half-car heated garage and workroom, which was hidden from the road. A large screened-in porch off the rear of the house overlooked a manicured lawn with hostas around a grouping of mature oak trees, beyond which was a pond. A pathway meandered down the hill, over a small wooden bridge where an old, dilapidated farmhouse, also part of the property, sat on the edge of an acre-and-a-half pond. The day we first visited, a tall blue heron sat on a submerged log—it was this bird in the picturesque setting that sold us on the property. "This is the type of place I envisioned. Far away from the hectic pace of the city!" I commented.

Despite the ugliness of the house, the landscape was enchanting. The woods were surrounded on all sides by working farmland. Beyond the pond was the boundary of the property, a gravel road that led both to the dilapidated farmhouse and to an old, blood-red barn. The barn likely had related to the old farmhouse at one time, but was now part of a neighbor's land, surrounded by paddocks that were used for dairy cows. The hilly rural road on which the property was situated just two miles outside of Gambier was seldom traveled, with the exception of an occasional pickup truck or an Amish buggy pulled by hitched horses. I had seen the magic Joe could make in transforming dilapidation into something special, so the 1970s A-frame wasn't a deterrent. We were sold.

For several years, we spent weekdays in our urban neighborhood just north of downtown Columbus while weekends were spent out in the country in Gambier, sometimes renovating but often just enjoying the surroundings. Joe designed a concept for the A-frame that opened the kitchen to the living room. We took out the overhead cabinets, the wall that had divided a small galley kitchen from the living room, and he built a large, elliptical-shaped island in its place. The top of the new eating area was a large-scale mosaic made from broken ceramic tiles, mainly white but also with bright yellow and a medium-gray tone to add color and contrast. The vertical surface below the island was corrugated metal. Cupboards and walls painted in a warm white, new carpeting in the living room, and a linoleum tile kitchen floor that played off the large eating island made a big difference in the house, with relatively minor effort and little cost.

After years of carefree living between construction projects, we were ready to start a family. We decided to remain in our current homes until our child was ready for school. Joe painted clouds in our guest room and commissioned his sculptor friend Ralph to fabricate two pieces of furniture for the baby's room, a dresser/changing table and a set of tall bookshelves. Ralph had been experimenting with colored epoxy, so the design featured a taupe-colored epoxy mixed with blue and pink in segments of the birch veneer furniture. The legs, which extended from the floor to the top of each piece, came from the same metal scrapyard where elements of the staircases were previously found. The top of dresser had a recess for a changing pad that would be able to change in the future. "After there is no longer a need for a changing table, we can retrofit a piece of glass over the recess to showcase valuables," Joe explained. Both pieces integrated indirect lighting into the design.

Within a year of the birth of our first child, I discovered I was pregnant with our second. With plans to remain in our homes, we discussed how the two children would share a bedroom for the first few years. One Sunday, after returning from our weekend home, we learned that the house across the street from ours had been hit by bullets that had originated from a high-rise a block away on High Street. The seven-story Columbus metropolitan housing building did not have a weapons policy. Despite neighborhood meetings with city officials requesting guns be removed from the facility, we were told that the residents were allowed to own guns just as we were. Many in our neighborhood were upset, and as a mother with a baby and another on the way, we thought perhaps now was the time to relocate to a neighborhood where we could raise our children without fear of gunfire.

Our realtor thought our modern renovation would be difficult to sell and might remain on the market for some time at the price point we were asking, so at eight months pregnant, with a sixteen-month-old toddler, we listed our house, assuming that the timing wouldn't be a problem. Within an hour of listing, we received an offer at full asking price, sending us scrambling to find a new house in a more child-friendly, inner-ring suburb.

CHAPTER 2:
Structure

I was very pregnant with my second child while chasing a toddler around the house all day and still managing my store, so searching for a new home was a welcome break from my hectic life. We had many friends living in the near east enclave of Bexley, home to Ohio's governor, Ohio State University's president, and many well-regarded educational institutions, so we decided to focus our search there. Drawn to the area for its excellent schools, its quality of residential architecture, and its close vicinity to downtown, the historic suburb has a quaint Main Street with trendy restaurants, an art deco arts theatre, and a forty-acre wooded park that would satisfy our appreciation of the outdoors. We loved trees, and Bexley had so many mature trees, it was nationally recognized as an arboretum. Knowing that raising children would occupy our time and that we would have less of it to maintain two residences, we decided to sell both of our properties so we could afford a house on a larger lot to make up for the loss of the weekend setting.

My friend Sarah accompanied me on tours as I attempted to weed out houses that I knew Joe would deplore. "Tiny useless rooms. Not enough light. No functional flow," I could already hear Joe complain about the average floor plan. If we were going to sell both properties, we needed to find a home Joe would like and one that could function without immediate renovation; I didn't want to live in a construction mess with two babies.

Joe's sculptor friend Ralph suggested we contact a man whose house had just featured an art sale that he attended. "It's a modern house with a flat roof," he told us, "once owned and designed by Noverre Musson, who was a Frank Lloyd Wright apprentice. Although it may be too small for you. The owner is retired and had the house on the market for three years but wasn't able to sell it. I think you'll like the inside." He provided us an address in the low-density north Bexley neighborhood, and we drove by that evening.

There were two houses next to each other that were obviously designed by the same architect, with the first one much smaller than the second. "It must be the smaller of the two, by Ralph's description," Joe said. "I love that it's located right across from the park. We can enjoy the beauty of the woods without us having to maintain it!" I replied back. Joe called the elderly gentleman and we set up a time to view the house. To our surprise, it was the larger of the two homes that he was interested in selling. "It's huge and across from that park. There is no way we can afford it, even after selling both of our properties," I commented. We had decided on a spending limit and I refused to budge. "Let's go find out," Joe countered.

The house was a symmetrical, two-story, flat-roofed mid-century modern with the second floor set back from the first floor. Below the roof line, an inverted triangle of a gable of sorts, painted Wright's signature Cherokee Red, seemed to point to the entrance. Two brick piers supported a beam that ran above the doorway, in front of which was a brick, semicircular, raised garden that concealed the steps to the entrance. The exterior was clad in warm mushroom-colored cedar shakes with expansive black posts and beams that defined the structure. We rang the doorbell, and a loud buzz that was startling to the ear caused us to jump.

An elderly man answered the door and invited us in. Carl, a former professional football player, had been a companion of Noverre Musson and was obviously attached to the house. He wanted to make sure the ownership was passed to someone who would appreciate the design and protect the property from developers who demolished houses on prominent sites in the landlocked suburb to build tasteless oversized houses known as McMansions, as was the trend.

The doorway opened to a tall atrium, and my eye was drawn immediately to a domed skylight, half the size of the room, that ascended to about fourteen feet. Ficus trees and other large plants filled the space, sitting in huge terra-cotta pots on the square brick floor as well as on raised wooden stands. The room was warm and humid, the perfect climate for the plants. "The skylight is removable and there are drains in the floor for water, in case you would want to open the room to the elements," Carl explained.

The atrium was divided from the rest of the house by the black structural framing infilled with glass and wooden shelves full of knickknacks. There were several brick steps up to French doors, through which a living room extended to the back of the house, terminating in another wall of glass and a pair of French doors leading to the backyard. Through the glass was an unobstructed view of deep green foliage.

"The house was planned as a series of eleven-foot square modules," Carl informed us, knowing Joe was an architect. "The living room is a double width module, twenty-two feet wide by forty-four feet to the rear. The atrium in front is a twenty-two by twenty-two-foot square, so you have a vista of sixty-six feet from the front to the back. On each side of the living room are eleven-foot-wide rooms extending the full length north to south," he further explained.

Just to the right as you entered the living room was a minimalist black steel spiral staircase, devoid of ornamentation, that led to the second floor. Beyond the open stairwell, which I secretly deemed a baby deathtrap, was the large open living room. The walls were lined in natural color burlap, faded over the years, with period furniture to match the era of the house. In the middle of the room, centered on a beam that traveled the length of the room, was another skylight, although this one was only about a four-foot square. Deep rose-color accordion wooden shutters, with a pink satin tapestry fabric in the inlay, framed the sliding doors along the back of the house. Similar folding doors, perhaps nine feet high, bordered the entrances to the rooms off the living room on both sides of the back of the room. "This is incredible.

Look at how those beams define the structure!" Joe exclaimed. Seeing that he instantly fell in love with the architecture, I started to worry that we would never be able to afford such a house and that he might never want to settle for another.

To the right of the living room was the kitchen and dining room, divided by sliding panels with a glass transom above. The ceilings were raised, and large clerestory windows ran along the entire length of the western exterior wall. A bay with windows on three sides created a breakfast nook. Off the kitchen toward the front of the house was a garage, one of two located on each side of the atrium. Their doors were discreetly camouflaged by the same cedar shakes that clad the rest of the house's exterior.

In between the kitchen and dining room was an open space with jewel-tone cabinetry on one side and another bay, this one with pedestals displaying artifacts. The dining room featured a Henredon Frank Lloyd Wright dining table and chairs that were last in production in the fifties, and long, low, attached shelving along the wall shared by the living room. My eye was drawn to a bright red silk kimono displayed against the deep teal of the western exterior wall. The end of the room overlooked lush gardens.

An extended roof covered the deck outside the rear doors and stepped down to limestone pavers. Pachysandra ground cover in square beds were framed by railroad ties on each side of the walk. Beyond the ground cover was a gridded concrete patio in crude exposed aggregate, with a cascading fountain made from two shallow, muted-yellow, fiberglass dishes, each about four feet wide, providing the soothing sound of trickling water. Limestone benches surrounded the patio with the arching branches of burning bushes that created a buffer from the adjoining yard. Despite the close vicinity of three gated communities on each side of the property, the mature trees and landscaping created a shield and gave the impression of being far removed from neighbors.

To the left of the back garden was a side yard large enough to fit another house, lined with mature oaks and maples. Linear gardens framed with railroad ties were meticulously groomed with purple and peach irises, lilies of the valley, and ivy. A concrete paver pathway led to the smaller of the two homes, with a six-foot fence enclosing both yards. "Noverre designed both of these houses, but the smaller is now owned by a pilot," Carl informed us. From out in the yard, we saw large piers extending from the ground, supporting a covered balcony off the second floor with a similar design on the west side of the house. "This is quite a majestic house," I commented. "Your grounds are likewise impressive. Do you have a gardener?" I asked, hoping that Joe would pick up on my fear that this property was over our price range. Carl commented that he enjoyed gardening and that he maintained his own yard.

Reentering the rear of the house, there were two bedrooms on the opposite side of the living room from the kitchen, each with its own carpeted bathroom that were mirror images of each other. As on the west facade, clerestory windows ran north to south, and each bedroom featured a sliding glass door to the outside.

Next to the front bedroom was a set of stairs that led to a walk-out basement that had served as Noverre's office for his architectural practice. Desks were still set up in rows, and there was a huge safe in a storage room toward the back.

As we climbed the spiral staircase from the living room, I worried how dangerous an open railing would be with two babies just eighteen months apart. I could tell Joe was becoming more attached to this house and I feared no other home would suffice. His comments repeatedly lauded the design and mentioned details that only an architect would notice on a first visit. "The upstairs," Carl explained, "was added in 1980 and rests on two glulam beams running the entire width of the house, extending out to create balconies on each end." "These are magnificent!" Joe exclaimed upon seeing the fifty-foot, twelve-foot by thirty-foot exposed beams of Douglas fir that transversed the entire floor east to west. The upstairs had two rooms—one a small bedroom on the west end with a tiny bathroom nestled behind accordion doors and a set of sliding doors leading to a balcony, and the other a large open sitting room, crowded with furniture and built-in bookshelves, appearing to be where Carl mainly resided. Sliding glass doors on the east also opened to a wood-decked balcony with access to the flat roof. Large, raised bay windows on both the north and south sides brought more light to the space as did another operable skylight in the center of the room. The entire second story, with views on all four sides, was surrounded with mature trees, providing the feeling you were in a tree house high up in the green branches.

We returned home and researched the property. Surrounded on three sides by gated communities, the two mid-century modern houses faced Jeffrey Woods, a forty-acre park that included the community swimming pool, tennis courts, and the 1905 Jacobethan Revival Jeffrey Mansion, a historic house donated to the city and used by the parks and recreation department. The two homes were designed by Noverre Musson, an architect who graduated from Ohio State University in 1932 and then apprenticed with Wright from 1935 to 1937. Musson had built the larger of the homes in 1964 for himself, and in the early 1980s, he had added the second small home at the same time as the house-spanning second story on the main house. Designed using the Wrightian principles of organic architecture, the house was secluded and sited to take advantage of gardens and mature trees.

After some negotiation, we purchased the house in January 1998, a couple months after the birth of our second child. "I love the house as much as you, but our first priority is to make it safe for a baby. There were probably never children in this house," I told Joe. "Maren is twenty-two months and Fia will be crawling before we know it!"

Over the next fifteen years, we renovated the house while raising our children in the idyllic setting. Joe did many of the improvements himself, with me again serving as an assistant. The spiral staircase was wrapped in plexiglass panels that he sanded to make translucent like rice paper, which allowed light but prevented toddlers from falls. He built an oak grid to fill an opening from the second floor to the kitchen where a skylight must have once been installed before the addition of the second floor. "I want to make sure it's strong enough in case a baby climbs down into it," I told Joe. So he climbed down, then jumped up and down to prove the oak-framed grid could support his or any baby's weight!

In place of burlap-covered walls, Joe installed medium density fiberboard (MDF) panels in the atrium and living room, leaving the thinnest of separation between panels for a minimalist detail. The original house lacked a fireplace, and with doors to the outside, we wondered if Noverre had a fear of fire, as the hearth was a central feature in Wrightian design. We felt the large open space needed the warmth of a fire, so Joe designed a fireplace for the atrium, using oak panels for a modern interpretation of a mantle, a concrete plinth, and panels made of acid-etched brass kickplates found at the scrapyard for the sides. We also installed a modern Finnish, soapstone-clad woodstove in the large living room to provide an extra element of coziness on cold days. Entertaining was important to us, and during our many large parties, the women guests would gather around the woodstove, enjoying the warmth that radiated from the stone.

In the kitchen, the water-damaged island was replaced by more functional granite, while the old butcher block was refinished and reused for tables in the bays of the kitchen and dining room. New appliances, more suitably sized for a family, replaced the old ones, and the shelving above the sink island was removed. We lost one cabinet from the dining room to enlarge the tiny bathroom to better suit our guests. Joe fabricated a concrete counter and added a stainless vessel bowl for a sink with a wall-mounted modern faucet. Being a mom, I noticed the modern lock system could be flipped, possibly locking children in the bathroom, so Joe added a floor-level window that could be accessed in an emergency.

In the dining room, Joe designed a sculptural ten-foot table in oak and oxidized steel, with an oblong bowl carved into the center. Ralph fabricated the large piece that was as beautiful underneath as it was on top. It took eight men to move it into place. It was a piece of art! After much searching, we decided on the iconic and comfortable Eames DCW chairs in ash for seating. Joe designed and built ash-veneer plywood wall panels and side cabinetry to complement the dining room set.

Both children's bathrooms were modernized, but special attention was given to the upstairs rooms that we intended for our personal suite. The small upstairs bedroom was transformed into a large open bathroom with a walk-in shower and toilet where the entire bathroom was originally placed. A travertine plinth that housed an air jet tub and two minimalist vessel sinks was built where the bed once sat. Two square pieces of oak veneer plywood were suspended on cables from the ceiling, featuring a round mirror on each with simple frosted-glass pendant light fixtures on each side. The large reading room was turned into a bedroom, where a platform bed that Joe had made years before was the only piece of furniture. Joe designed and commissioned Ralph to build a long wall of built-in closets and concealed drawers that rested on one of the glulam beams, appearing to float off the wall. The room, with expansive windows in each direction, was like being in a tree house. The kids loved going up there during violent thunderstorms, hiding under the covers of our bed when the loud crashes of thunder resonated. During the summer months, the shade from the mature trees and the cross flow from the open screens kept the room comfortable so we could enjoy the cheerful sounds of children playing at the pool across the street.

Although the house had only three bedrooms, it had over 5,000 square feet, great for active children and large gatherings. But as our children approached college age, we dreamed of building a smaller modern house on the empty lot we owned that separated the two existing Musson houses. During our older child's senior year, we went to the considerable effort to legally split the lot and started to design a smaller house that would be better suited for our aging bodies in anticipation of becoming empty nesters. We sold the large house and temporarily rented the smaller of the two houses, which sat vacant at the time.

CHAPTER 3:
Discovering Glenbrow

In September of 2013, our oldest daughter, Maren, was taking an AP Studio Art class during her senior year of high school to help create a portfolio to use for admission to study architecture. She had developed a theme of "Urban Ruins" that incorporated her interest in photography with her passion for exploring abandoned buildings. Since entering unsecured structures can be a dangerous venture, I insisted on accompanying her in an attempt to keep her out of harm's way.

Years before, Joe's sculptor friend Ralph had forwarded us a local newspaper article about an attempt by local preservationists and the kin of one of the home's architects to save a house designed by apprentices of Frank Lloyd Wright known as the Gunning House. The house, built of cypress and stone, was located on a ravine on the east side of Columbus. "You guys should go out and look at this house," Ralph told us, but it was the depth of winter, and we were working on our own house and our lives were occupied with raising our children. Still, knowing the house was situated on a road we traveled to attend cross-country and swimming meets, we casually searched from the car's windows over the years, but to no avail.

It was the memory of the article, coupled with a search for a possible "urban ruin" for Maren to photograph, that led me to scan the roadside as we traveled to a hardware store out east. I knew the house was located about two miles outside the outer belt on a stretch of road with fifty-mile-per-hour speed limits. Ralph had told us that the property was adjacent to a suburban tract development, now ubiquitous to the once idyllic farmland outside the perimeters of many midwestern cities. On that afternoon, as we passed a residential area, I noticed an extended grove of trees with a commercial "For Sale" sign. A driveway broke through a small opening in the overgrown trees, grapevines dangling overhead. In the split second we passed, I glimpsed a flat roof and exclaimed, "I found it!" "Found what?" Joe replied. "That apprentice house that Ralph told us to check out. It might be perfect for Maren to photograph and there's a 'For Sale' sign."

Joe turned the car around, and as we drove through the opening, it was like traveling to another time and place. We left behind the suburban hell of modern America and ventured into a serene, picturesque woodland and meadow that had begun the process of reclaiming its man-made structures. We parked in front of a long four-bay carport cluttered with piles of decayed leaves and the remnants of former owners.

We exited the car and walked into an area of knee-deep prairie grass in what once must have been a manicured lawn in order to get a better view of the entire property. In front of us was a pond with two large gray boulders next to the water's edge—a thick, rose-colored, horizontal line transversed through both. The far side of the pond was marked by cascading boulders scattered on a hill beyond, blocked from the roadway by dense trees. Despite being overgrown with tall cattails, a large patch of waterlilies added a bright accent, speckled by dashing dragonflies in periwinkle and black. Across the water on a partially submerged boulder, two black entangled snakes warmed themselves in the autumn sun. As I watched, one slowly slid its lissome body into the dark reflective surface and gracefully disappeared behind the aquatic plants. Schools of goldfish below the surface scattered as giant bullfrogs leaped into the water, chirping on our approach. Idyllic! It was as if we had traveled to paradise. We sat on the two large boulders on the water's edge, shaded by the dappled light cast by the draping branches of several river birch trees, and took in the view.

As we took in the view from the boulders, we noticed something looming over the carport, densely covered in vine. "What is that?" Joe asked. As we walked back past the car bays, we realized there was a tall tower just beyond the carport that had been hidden by the overgrowth of English ivy. A red-framed entrance, with four, square, vertical windows next to a wooden screen door left ajar, revealed a "No Trespassing" sign. The tower was perched on a steep ravine edge, rising four stories to its top. The entire building was so enveloped in vines, it appeared like a huge topiary, virtually disappearing into the wooded backdrop behind the buildings. "This is attached to the carport, which is attached to the walkway and house, so it must be part of the property," Joe explained. "Oh my God, this is so incredibly cool!"

On the near side of the carport was what appeared to be a storeroom full of trash bags, emptied drawers, and dried leaves, with partially collapsed fragments of the roof hanging down from the ceiling. Off the storeroom, an attached covered walkway, in an advanced state of deterioration, cascaded down over pairs of concrete paver steps, leading down to a long, flat-roofed house that was so low to the ground it appeared to be growing directly out of the soil.

We returned to the yard, avoiding the covered walkway, which had partially collapsed from a large tree branch puncturing through to create a gaping hole. The branch had broken off of an aged black locust tree with three thick stems extending from its base. Vines grew along the base, covering portions of the walkway. Black tar paper dangled along with vines from the roof that extended over the steps that led to the house. At the end of the steps, the main house was situated several feet below the ground plane with a sunken courtyard in both the front and side. Another mature tree, heavily covered in vines and surrounded with bramble, sat directly in front of what appeared to be a main entrance. Fallen branches tangled in overgrown weeds prevented us from approaching the front door. The house was sided in horizontal rows of alternating wide and narrow boards, weathered gray from neglect, exaggerating the length of the long, low dwelling. "The siding is called board-and-batten and was used by Frank Lloyd Wright in his Usonian homes," Joe explained. "I wonder if that weathered wood is cypress." Above the board- and-batten siding, there was a row of clerestory windows, above which a thin soffit extended from the flat roof. A wood door in a rich golden hue, marred by deep animal scratches, was located at the junction of a stone wall. "That must have been the main entrance, and the siding must have matched that wood at one time but has been weathered to a gray patina," Joe added.

The roughly cut stone wall that framed the side of the door rose up to meet a raised section of roof. Another row of clerestory windows lined the raised portion just below the roofline, with another lower row of horizontal windows at waist height. A gray weathered trellis, leaning due to age and neglect, extended out beneath the upper clerestory windows and was topped with sagging plastic panels. The trellis covered a patio layered in years of dried mud and stone that obviously had cascaded down from a collapsed retaining wall that had once separated the lower patio from the raised lawn above.

We made our way down a set of four stone steps at the end of the house to a narrow glass door, left partially ajar, that was around the corner from the waist-high strip of windows. We peered inside the dark interior, but the entrance was blocked by wood panels and moldy pink fiberglass insulation. Spider webs coated with grime blocked the opening, and as we peered inside, a large brown spider disappeared into a deep webbed funnel at the edge of the doorway. "Yikes! I think I'll pass on going inside," I said, quickly backing away.

"This house must have been magnificent in its day," Joe exclaimed. "Maybe we should buy it?" I suggested. Joe lowered his chin gave me a look over the top of his glasses. "Well, regardless," I replied back, "it's perfect for Maren to photograph for her portfolio."

As we walked back toward the car, we noticed small hints of its past splendor. Bright magenta crocuses and the aubergine leaves of a Japanese maple peeked out from beneath the twisted overgrowth. We took note of the realtor as we ventured back to the dreary reality of late capitalism's suburban sprawl.

We returned home to the smaller of the Noverre Musson houses that we were renting while we planned to build a new house on the lot next door. I called the realtor to find out if we could view the house. He told me the 2.38-acre property, listed for $297,000, was being sold for commercial land only. "The buildings are in terrible shape," I was told. I explained our situation and how Joe had restored several homes in the past and asked whether we could view the inside of the buildings. "Yes, go ahead! The house is unlocked" he told me, assuming we were yet another group of architecture enthusiasts just wanting to view the buildings.

By weird coincidence, after I got off the phone with the realtor, there was a knock on the door. A man introduced himself as Bill Schottenstein, a name I recognized as a local real estate developer. Bill had seen our children's athletic signs with "Kuspan Cross-Country" in front of the house and asked if Joe Kuspan lived here. He commented that he knew my husband from a city planning board that they both had served on and thought we lived next door. I explained that we had split the double lot and had just sold the house with plans to build a new house on the lot between the two houses. "You own the empty lot?" he asked. "Are you willing to sell it?" I told him that by coincidence, we had just returned from viewing an abandoned property we might be interested in and that I would have Joe contact him. Auspicious?

Shortly after, my kids, Maren and Fia, returned from cross-country practice, famished as usual. "Dinner is almost ready, so lay off the snacks," I told them as they headed straight to the cupboard. "After dinner we're going to photograph a cool abandoned building Dad and I discovered today," I told them, without mentioning my newfound interest in it. The kids, both aspiring architects and avid photographers, were contributing to the design of their living spaces in the planning of the new house, so knowing the condition of the property, I thought their interest would be confined to using the site for photography.

After dinner we headed out east, both kids with their respective cameras. On the way, I provided a short history on what we knew about the house, mainly based on a newspaper article from several years ago. "The house was designed by Wright apprentices, but much earlier than our Noverre Musson house. It sat abandoned for many years. Ralph had told us about it years ago, but we just discovered it today on our way to pick up floor adhesive. It should be a perfect site for Maren's studio art project," I explained.

The sun was much lower on the horizon when we arrived after dinner, casting long dark shadows from the towering evergreens in the front of the house onto the upper lawn. Maren disappeared with her camera as we wandered the grounds. An opening between the evergreens and the tree line along the road revealed an abandoned tennis court, so far removed from use that twenty-foot trees were growing out of upheaved cracks in the green court pavement. Rusted net posts remained at the center edges of the court, while tall, rusted poles that used to hold the perimeter fence stood at each end, draped in vines. "Be careful where you step! Remember . . . leaves of three, let them be," I reminded Fia. Fallen branches covered in poison ivy and honeysuckle lay strewn across the court, likely from another tall black locust just behind the perimeter fence's skeleton. Despite its advanced stage of deterioration, the court, surrounded by tall prairie grass, goldenrod, and aster still held a charm.

"Mom, come and look at this," Maren called out to us. Holding onto the stone wall, I looked around the corner to see Maren standing on a stone planter jutting out high above a sloped glen, aiming her camera at the far end of the building. The house was situated on the precipitous edge of a ravine, with a steep decline in topography that made me hesitate proceeding. "I'll pass. I prefer to keep my feet safely planted on terra firma. I'll see your photos later. We're about to go inside. Come join us," I replied back.

We peeked into the house, but the dense foliage that surrounded the structure, coupled with the setting sun, left the mahogany-colored interior dark and foreboding. Joe pushed away the webs with a stick and we stepped over the soggy insulation into a galley kitchen. The terra-cotta-colored concrete floor had a layer of dried mud from previous flooding. Jewel-toned kitchen cabinets had been pulled away from the walls. "Thieves have gone after the copper pipes," Joe commented. In front of us was the stone wall that extended up to meet the clerestory windows that lined the edge of the raised ceiling—they were bringing in little light in the early evening in the shadows of the dense evergreens. On the back side of the kitchen, another stone wall extended up to the raised ceiling with an angled fireplace that served both the open kitchen and the adjacent room. In this open space adjoining the kitchen, a row of French doors brought a verdant view of the ravine that was scattered with trees in which thick vines crept upward from the soil. A stone planter projected off of an adjacent room with a vine covered trellis above. The land sloped sharply downward, but overgrown bramble and grapevines dangling from tree branches prevented a view of the creek below. "See that gridded pattern cut into the concrete floor—I'm guessing it's two by four?" Joe noted, "That's another Wrightian detail that was used as a construction module for laying out the building."

Beyond this room was a bedroom with dark wood-paneled walls and boarded-up windows. An opening for an air conditioning unit, most likely stolen, exposed the house to the elements. Around the corner was a small bathroom with a walk-in, stone-walled shower. "This would be a safe place if a tornado hit," Joe commented. "Eew," cried Fia, quickly backing away, "it's full of cobwebs! I'd rather face a tornado!"

Off the kitchen, beyond the angled fireplace, was a hallway that stepped down to the room that extended to a point high above the ravine, like the prow of a ship. Through a bank of French doors, the lush greenery of vines that were growing on a trellis just outside had begun creeping through cracks as it extended into the interior as well. The small room, which must have been an office or perhaps a bedroom, had a second stone fireplace and a raised platform, on which sat an empty modern desk and chair. "This fireplace is part of the same stone structure as the one in the kitchen," Joe commented, "it must share a chimney." Accordion wood doors led to a small bathroom with stone walls and a raised ceiling with windows at the high ceiling. The room contained closets, stacked drawers, and was divided into three sections: one with a vanity missing its sink and faucet, one with an old bathtub in a soft coral color, and the last a small alcove with a toilet. A handmade ladder that matched the modern aesthetics was perched against the wall.

As the sun continued to set, it was becoming darker, so we quickly toured the rest of the house. A small passage to the left of the entrance led to a large room with three bays of stacked horizontal windows along the ravine, each separated by a robust pier of stacked stone; a built-in sofa covered with loose ceiling panels and piles of cellulose insulation; and a third stone fireplace angled from the wall. The ceilings were low and dark, with a band of horizontal clerestory windows along the front of the house, bringing only slight relief to the dark space.

Beyond the sofa was an open room with an obviously sagging ceiling supported by four foot by four-foot posts. "Don't mess with those posts, they look to be keeping the roof structure from total collapse!" Joe commented. Large, fixed, plate glass windows, different from the rest of the house, lined the walls opening to the ravine. A stone wall, similar to the rest of the house and marked with a vertical line where a wall must have divided the space, stood between the groupings of windows on the ravine side. The concrete floor had marks where the wall must have stood, as well as protruding gas lines—perhaps once used to heat the space. On the wall opposite the ravine were drainpipes for plumbing along with a dingy curtain that had once been used to cover this section. At the far side of the room was an overgrown sunken courtyard formed by the entry walkway and the raised ground of the carport. "Hmm, this section appears to have been finished later than the rest of the house," Joe mused, noting the difference in windows. "It's getting dark, and we don't have a flashlight," I reminded him.

As the sun was setting, we headed back to the car, amazed at our discovery. "Can we buy it?" Fia asked. Despite the condition, its charm and potential were apparent even to our daughters. "This place is really cool!" Maren commented. "I got some great shots!"

That night, as I lay awake in bed, my mind was transfixed with thoughts of our discovery. There was something so enchanting about nature reclaiming this piece of organic architecture—back to the land from where it once rose. Still, at one time, this house must have been thriving with life, loved by the family who inhabited it. Laughter and tears, celebrations and disappointments. Every human emotion had filled the walls, but time had passed. The house had grown silent and before long, the elements took their toll. Perhaps it was best to let nature take its course; the flora and fauna seemed to prefer it. I knew that the bliss of nature was to be short-lived as sprawl had crept to the edges of the property. If we didn't buy it, I could only imagine the bulldozers and asphalt paving, and soon after, "The Shoppes at Glenbrow Ravine" would appear. Ugh! We needed to save this property!

CHAPTER 4:

Offer Accepted!

The first thing the next morning, I called the realtor to tell him we were interested in the property but would want to restore the house as well. Joe would bring an engineer to assess the underlying structural integrity of the house before we were willing to make an offer. I explained that we had sold our house and were willing to make a cash offer if the engineer deemed it structurally sound. After years of hearing excitement from other potential buyers, the agent wasn't convinced and referred me to an assistant, Elaine. Elaine explained that many people had expressed interest over the years, but most had simply wanted a chance to view the house. Those who were interested backed away after seeing the project was not financially viable and had too many unknowns. The second owners had passed away, leaving it to a relative, who had also passed away, leaving it to a niece. "The current owner was out of town and not willing to provide any maintenance," she told us. Reinforcing what the earlier article had informed me, Elaine told me the house was last inhabited in 2006 with virtually no maintenance since that time.

Joe contacted his structural engineer friend, Rick Geers, who agreed to assess the condition of the house for any major problems. Thieves had dropped several ceiling panels and cabinets were pulled away from the wall in search of copper, so they had some access to portions of the underlying structure. There was extensive water and insect damage as we expected, but the house wasn't about to collapse into the ravine. The entire roof would need to be replaced, including the sheathing, with major portions needing to be completely restructured. Only after all the ceiling and wall panels were removed could the full extent of the damage be assessed. The entire heating and plumbing system would need to be replaced as well. On a brighter note, the house had stood for nearly seventy-five years, so obviously it was well-built.

The damage in the tower was far worse, despite it being over twenty years younger. It was filled with black mold from years of water penetration and deterioration caused by both animals and insects. The window along the ravine side of the tower was missing a few pieces of glass. The framing for the glass was also acting as the structural support for the floor and roof beams along that side and was not badly damaged, keeping that side from collapse.

The average person would have been frightened away by the immense task of restoring the house with its list of unknown costs and ancillary structures in need of extensive work. Having been through four house renovations in various forms of distress, as well as two storefront transformations with Joe, I was convinced of his ability to transform this jewel back to its former glory.

Revisiting estimates from the earlier *Columbus Dispatch* article that Joe's friend Ralph had sent, for our initial budget, we more than doubled the previous high-end estimates for repair and added that number to the price we were willing to pay. Although we assumed it would be sufficient, we could tap into the equity of the other house we purchased to live in during restoration. We had good credit, so we also assumed it would not be difficult to get a short-term mortgage should the need arise. After several exchanges, our cash offer was accepted, and we hoped to close by Thanksgiving. In the meantime, we were allowed to seal up the property at our expense and remove vegetation that covered the buildings.

We soon had bad news from Elaine: "The property had federal tax liens attached to it and was about to go to auction." By this point, I had my heart set on restoring the Gunning House; building new on a suburban lot would no longer suffice. Knowing that foreign speculators were buying up distressed properties, and fearing a local developer might decide to express interest in the property, which would start a bidding war, we were at the mercy of the government. We were forced to wait over the winter and spring for the court's decision.

In the meantime, we gutted, renovated, and moved into a small house that was in foreclosure on the other side of Bexley near Capital University, in order to remain in the school district for our younger daughter's final years of high school. The temporary house was an uninspiring 1970s split-level—near the library and Main Street—that most would consider in very poor shape, but I thought we would turn a sizable profit after our future house was ready to move into.

CHAPTER 5:
Chronicle

During the long winter months, as we awaited the court decision, I researched everything I could find about the property. The house was known as the Gunning House, but the original Gunning family referred to it as Glenbrow, a name given to it by the original designers. It was designed by two apprentices of Frank Lloyd Wright, Tony Smith and Laurence Cuneo, and another young designer, Ted van Fossen. The three had met at the New Bauhaus located in Chicago, a school headed by Lázló Moholy-Nagy, an emigrant from the original Bauhaus School in Dessau, Germany. The program closed after only a year, following a "student revolt" over a change in the expected curriculum. Robert Storr, the Museum of Modern Art curator for the 1998 exhibition, *Tony Smith: Architect, Painter, Sculptor*, provided some excellent background along with research and essays by John Keenan and Joan Pachner in the accompanying catalogue. Storr stated that Moholy-Nagy's emphasis on "scientific design" triggered protests that led to the school's closing after that first year.

After leaving the program, Cuneo convinced Smith to visit the construction site of Frank Lloyd Wright's Suntop Homes, in Ardmore, Pennsylvania. Designed as a four-unit, multistory building, the individual residences pinwheeled around an inner courtyard, providing both privacy and views of nature. Having recently read Wright's autobiography, the site impressed the two enough to join the Taliesin Fellowship as apprentices while van Fossen worked as a laborer alongside them.

After working on the Suntop Homes, Smith was elevated to "Clerk of the Works" by Wright, who placed him in charge of the next project the trio worked on—the Andrew F. H. Armstrong House in Ogden Dunes, Indiana. This Usonian house from 1939 consisted of two floors positioned at a thirty-degree shift from each other, with a four-by-four-foot grid imprinted into the concrete floors that related to the shift. Parts of the main level reference the thirty-degree shift of the floor above while maintaining their own floor grid arrangement. This shift appears to have subsequently influenced the plans for the Gunning House, with its superimposed thirty-degree degree shifts, although they all only occurred on the floor level.

Ted van Fossen grew up in Columbus, Ohio, attending the University High School that was located on the campus of the Ohio State University. There he met and befriended a young journalist and his wife, Rob and Mary Gunning. The Gunnings were a young bohemian Quaker couple who enjoyed long intellectual discussions with Ted, often centering on art and architecture, as well as their shared interest in traveling. After a bike tour through France and England in the late 1930s, they approached their young friend, then only nineteen years old, to help them select a piece of property for them and to design a home on the site. "They would load me into a Willys (the early pre-war name for what would come to be called a Jeep) to take me to various pieces of land for me to give them my opinion of each site for their house," said Ted.

During one such outing, the trio drove out east on Broad Street, past the grand houses near Franklin Park Conservatory, the growing village of Bexley, and out to rolling farmland, several miles past what would eventually become Route 270, the outer belt of Columbus.

They stopped at a partially wooded site in Blacklick owned by the Cady family. Ted told them he thought this should be their site: "The house could be designed to marry the open field with the wooded ravine along the complete break that existed between them. It would face south into the view of the ravine drinking in the sun in the winter and being protected from it in the summer."

The Gunnings told Ted that they liked the French farmhouses they had encountered on their bicycle tours in France. They made one stipulation:

"The house should not have a flat roof like the modern architecture that they encountered during their travels."

Ted van Fossen was astonished that Rob and Mary would entrust such a young man. He wrote to his good friends Tony Smith and Larry Cuneo, working on Wright's Usonian Armstrong House in Ogden Dunes, Indiana, with news of the commission, requesting they should come directly to Columbus. This was a huge break for the young men, as Tony Smith was twenty-seven years old while both van Fossen and Cuneo were each nineteen years of age.

Smith had the most experience of the three, having trained as a mechanical draftsman for his family's factory, A. P. Smith Manufacturing, a company that specialized in toolmaking and that was well-known for fabricating fire hydrants. During an apprenticeship at the factory, Smith learned the use of the lathe and drill press. His skills were further developed working as an apprentice under Wright in 1938 and 1939, first as a carpenter's assistant and bricklayer, though later, he was promoted to overseeing the role as project manager in what the Taliesin Fellowship deemed "Clerk of the Works."

The apprenticeship was centered on Wright's principles of organic architecture: integrating a building into its natural environment so that it is in harmony with the landscape, the use of locally sourced materials, the role of proportion and scale, and finally, that the building should provide both shelter and inspiration. The young men, under the spell of working with Frank Lloyd Wright's philosophy, were thrilled to have such an opportunity to test their knowledge and create a building based on Wright's principles.

After receiving word of the Gunning commission, Smith and Cuneo headed to Columbus to meet with their new clients and work out a design for the house. Their first obstacle was to sell their design to Rob and Mary Gunning. "It was not a French farmhouse and it did not even have a sloping roof. In order to freely arrange the spaces and provide the best views of the ravine, a flat roof was dictated to keep costs down," van Fossen later wrote.

The design featured an open kitchen where Mary would be at the center of activity instead of shut out like a servant. Views of the ravine from the dining and living space would have little visual separation from the beauty of the outdoors. "What we had done was to rework the old farmhouse kitchen in a modern architectural way," van Fossen wrote.

Just three years after Wright's first Usonian house known as Jacobs I (now a World Heritage site) was completed, the young men incorporated a great many elements of Wright's Usonian principles to design a modern functional house that brought the beauty of the wooded ravine into the living spaces of the house. Smith approached the design philosophically, as he did much in his life:

> This marks the planting of the city in this country place.
> It is an addition, not a growth.
> It is related to the whole as a 4th element & in terms of measure
> the original unity is three fold from a common center.
> this does not, however, spring from the center, nor does
> it grow from one of the wings, it stands
> apart and yet
> is an element of a new unity based on number or measure
> this is a very urbane attitude
> it marks the beginning of a specifically human institution
> as opposed to a natural or organic unity.

The house the young designers presented to the Gunnings was a single-story, flat-roofed house that snaked along the edge of the ravine to allow vistas of the meandering creek and wooded glen. The building would emerge out of a sunken entry court, low to the ground, and it would appear to grow from the earth along the southern edge of the ravine. The exterior of the house would be clad in horizontal cypress board-and-batten siding as well as stone that had been quarried on site. A rough-cut stone wall would frame one side of the main entrance, rising above the level of the main roof to provide a raised ceiling for the kitchen area. Clerestory windows lined three walls of the upper section with a counter-level strip of windows running its entire length below.

On the side facing the ravine, French doors lined the south elevation of the house, jutting out at an angle to aim true south. This extended "Point Room" would be embellished by a cantilevering stone planter below additional sets of French doors. East of the Point Room would be three massive stone piers with bands of horizontal stacked windows between the piers. This room was called the dormitory, intended for use as a children's bedroom. At the far end of the house would be an angled attached carport, parallel to the angle of the point room, with an elongated stone pier supporting the roof.

The central core would house three fireplaces: one facing the kitchen/living room, one in the bedroom that the Gunning's dubbed the Point Room, and one in children's dormitory. The floor plan they proposed was revolutionary in Columbus, Ohio, at the time. Borrowing from Wright's Usonian floor plan, which opened the kitchen to both the dining and living spaces, the plan would allow Mary's workspace (Wright's term for the kitchen) to be an active part of her family's activities. Past the kitchen fireplace would be a short hallway that stepped down to Rob and Mary's bedroom. An elevated platform to position their bed (actually back on the main level of the house) would provide a commanding view of the wooded hillside and creek below. To the left of the front entrance would be the dormitory—a large room for the children with built-in storage and beds placed between the stone piers. To help defray costs, the house would offer built-in furniture, eliminating most of their need to purchase it.

After the long explanation of the proposed plan, Rob turned to Mary and asked, "What do you think of it?" "I don't understand anything about how it will look, but if it works like all the consideration they have given to how we will live in it, I think I like it!" Rob replied, "I think I like it too."

The young designers were ecstatic. They poured their hearts into building their creation using the trades and experience gained through working with Wright. Their youthful energy, aided by inexpensive labor during the waning years of the Depression, helped keep their project on schedule and within the budget set by the Gunnings. The house design was so unique in Columbus that upon completion, the tax assessor thought they were living in the basement until the couple could afford to build the real house on top of it!

Rob and Mary moved into their new house by January of 1941. So moved by the results, Mary wrote to Tony Smith, "It is such a beautiful house and living in it is so good. I feel a debt to you—and Ted all my life long. I never get through with the joy of looking and there is always a quiet and a peace and yet a deep excitement. I wish I could put into words all the things I see and feel about this house but I don't have the words." Rob was taken by the house as well, hurrying home to work on small projects around the house. As Mary wrote Smith, "You must know that this is your home too—and for Ted, too. I think the making of something like this home is something that belongs to you that will never be lost. It will be here waiting and there are plenty of beds in the dormitory." She tells Smith to give her "regards to Ted and tell him that those parts of the house where books are kept and where we sit and work and keep things are really beautiful."

By September of 1942, Rob and Mary's first child, Nora, was born. In a letter from Rob to Tony, the proud father describes, "Things go very well with us and we seem to have a happier and happier life. We wish you would come out for a visit, get acquainted with Nora and make us all even happier." As the family continued to grow, the desire for more room led Rob and Mary to consider expanding their small house.

Although the Gunnings remained in correspondence with both Tony Smith and Ted van Fossen, the latter pair had moved out west to California, mingling with an artistic crowd centered around the Frank Lloyd Wright-designed Hollyhock guest house in Los Angeles known as Residence B of Olive Hill. Ted van Fossen and Larry Cuneo were sent overseas during World War II, while Tony Smith, excused from serving due to health reasons, married Jane Lawrence, an opera singer, in 1943—playwright Tennessee Williams served as the best man. Jane is reported to have inspired the character of Blanche Dubois in Williams's *A Streetcar Named Desire*. I discovered photographs of both Smith and van Fossen, along with Smith's wife, Jane Lawrence, taken by the Los Angeles-based avant-garde photographer Edmund Teske, in the book *Spirit into Matter*. Teske had briefly taught at the New Bauhaus in Chicago and worked for Frank Lloyd Wright as well, setting up a photographic studio at Taliesin in Wisconsin.

During this period, Ted van Fossen married Maggie Belgrano, a Stanford University dance major who was the practice partner of famed actor and dancer Gene Kelly. Maggie Belgrano van Fossen came from a wealthy San Francisco family—her father was Frank N. Belgrano Jr., the president of Transamerica Corporation, and her distant cousin, Manuel Belgrano, was a founder of the nation of Argentina. By the late 1940s, Ted and Maggie had a son whom they named Tony.

There are several letters of correspondence between Robert Gunning and Tony Smith regarding the late 1940s enclosure of the original carport, but it is unclear whether distance made the project too difficult. With Smith in New York and van Fossen in California, the Gunnings turned to another Taliesin apprentice residing in Columbus, Noverre Musson, to develop and execute the design. By weird coincidence, it was in Noverre Musson's house that we raised our children, in nearby Bexley. Musson's 1948 plans for the Gunnings includes the enclosure of the original attached carport, converting the space into two small children's bedrooms with a small bathroom and laundry room. The windows he added were large, fixed plate glass units that provided ample light, but the only ventilation was from operable horizontal screened ledges separating the top and bottom pieces of offset plate glass. Attached to this newly enclosed space was a covered walkway ascending to the driveway with steps of paired, precast twenty-four-inch-by-twenty-four-inch concrete pavers beneath.

Musson's facade emphasized the vertical more than the house did, employing a series tall window openings and piers as well as using stucco for the exterior instead of the cypress board-and-batten siding. Seven stuccoed piers supported the roof of the walkway with wall sconce fixtures in each pier to illuminate the path. The first four piers ascended up the steps while the final three piers, each seven feet tall, defined the enclosed space of the carport with windows in between. At the end of the walkway, he attached a structure with a workroom and a tiny seven-by-four-foot guest room known to the Gunnings as the Monk's Cell. Beyond the enclosed part of the structure, he extended two carport bays for vehicles.

By 1951, Ted van Fossen's marriage had ended, and he returned to central Ohio and reignited his friendship with the Gunnings, initially moving into the tiny Monk's Cell at Glenbrow. By 1954, van Fossen formed a partnership with local developers and Wright enthusiasts, Martha and Dick Wakefield, focusing his design career on the creation of Rush Creek Village in Worthington, Ohio, in what came to be the largest community of Usonian-style homes based on Wright's principles of organic architecture. The partnership lasted several decades and resulted in nearly fifty homes designed by Ted van Fossen. In 2003, Rush Creek Village was listed on the National Registry of Historic Places.

Tony Smith had returned to New York where he taught at NYU, Cooper Union, Hunter College, and Pratt Institute until he departed for Germany so that his wife, Jane, could pursue her career in opera. During his time in Europe, Tony focused on painting and upon his return to the States, he resumed teaching and began his career in art, creating his first sculpture in 1956 as he and Jane started a family, eventually having three daughters: Kiki, Seton, and Beatrice. (It was Kiki and Seton Smith who later visited the house to advocate for its purchase that led to our knowledge of the property).

Dismayed over dealing with clients, Smith abandoned architecture after completing only about twenty buildings. A 1966 interview between Tony Smith and Samuel Wagstaff Jr., the art curator and collector, for *Artforum* magazine includes a photograph of Glenbrow over the caption, "*House for Robert Gunning,*" Black Lick (*sic*), Ohio, 1940, the first house built by Tony

Smith and the one most influenced by Wright. Wright saw it and liked it."

Gaining recognition and acclaim for his large, three-dimensional geometric pieces, Tony Smith was photographed beneath one of his pieces, *Smoke*, for the cover of *Time* magazine in 1967 under the caption, "Master of the Monumentalists." Smith was awarded a prestigious Guggenheim Fellowship in 1968, and later, the American Institute of Architects (AIA) awarded him their Fine Arts Medal for his influence in architecture in 1971.

Little is known about Larry Cuneo other than he was briefly married to apprentice Kay Schneider prior to the Gunning commission and that he served as the art director for the first season of the *I Love Lucy* television series.

Both a journalist and an author, Robert Gunning collaborated with his wife, Mary, in 1952 to develop a test, known as the Gunning FOG Index, that was used in newspaper and textbook publishing to ensure that a given text was appropriate for the intended reading audience. In the early 1960s, as Robert's success grew, the Gunnings decided to further expand the footprint of the house and also add an additional structure for an office and workspace. With Tony Smith focused on his artwork, and because Ted had returned to the area and gained experience in the design of many houses at Rush Creek Village, Ted was given the project at Glenbrow.

The main house was to add another bedroom and bathroom on the western end of the structure, as well as a modest expansion to the kitchen that included an outdoor patio outside the kitchen door. A set of French doors from "the lounge" were removed and relocated so that the new bedroom would have exterior access to the ravine. Large panels of plate glass filled the place where the previous doors had been positioned. Beyond the newly extended wall of glass to the new bedroom, van Fossen used mitered plate glass to form a seamless corner window overlooking the ravine—a design element learned from Wright. A framed glass door exited from the new bedroom onto the other side to the new kitchen patio. The attached bathroom featured a small, stone-walled, walk-in shower, a cypress butcher block vanity, a toilet, and a waist-high corner window for ventilation that viewed the majestic spruces outside.

The new separate structure that Ted van Fossen designed to be used as office space for Robert Gunning was an intriguing concept—a four-story tower attached to an expanded carport, with two automobile bays added (for a total of four). The tower would have three floors of living space and a roof terrace on the top. Built into the ravine, it would have stucco walls and a vertical band of square, jewel-tone glass windows extending the height of the building to provide filtered daylight for the enclosed stairwell. The ravine side of each floor would extend outward with windows in three directions, mitered glass at the corners, which would provide commanding views of the glen and creek below.

The lowest level would be partially belowground, the remnants of an earlier structure housing a small kiln for Mr. Gunning's dabbling into clay sculpture, and would have a worktable facing the windows to admire the view. The second level would be the main entrance level that would house Robert Gunning's office. On the third floor would be a guest bedroom and bathroom also featuring vertical panes of both colored and clear glass. Sunlight filtering through the colored squares would create prisms on the parquet floor. The top level would be a roof terrace with an extended trellis above. A closet on the open-aired terrace would conceal a Murphy bed for sleeping under the stars on hot summer nights before air conditioning was common.

The Gunnings were impressed with this design, standing tall against the backdrop of mature hardwoods that lined the hillside. Upon completion, they hosted one of their large parties to honor Ted's efforts and to show off their new living and working spaces.

The years passed, and the children grew up and moved away to begin their own life journeys. Robert Gunning passed away from complications of ALS in March 1980. Instead of a solemn funeral, he requested his life be celebrated with a party for their friends. A celebration of Robert's life was held at Glenbrow with family, friends, and colleagues. The event was memorialized in the *Akron Beacon Journal*, a former employer, in a six-page article, "Robert Gunning's Last Party," which described the gathering:

"Instead of a funeral, the family and friends of a much beloved man celebrate a life well lived."

Mary continued to live in her beloved home until her death in 1986. Ted van Fossen wrote and delivered a moving eulogy for Mary upon her death. "Mary had that quiet radiant beauty in which her intellect, indeed her whole spirit spoke," he remembered.

CHAPTER 6:
Decline

Fritz and Rebecca Neuenschwander purchased Glenbrow in 1990 and lived there until 2006. During their ownership, they removed the original cabinetry and butcher block counters in the kitchen, replacing them with plastic laminate in jewel-tone colors and faux marble counters. The wall that divided the original carport to form the two small children's bedrooms was removed, causing a noticeable sag in the ceiling. Support posts were later added to prevent the roof from collapsing.

On the outside, a concrete pool had been filled in and replaced with a small pond in front of the tree line that screened Broad Street. The earth was mounded behind the pond, and large boulders that were brought in appear to have once featured a waterfall that cascaded down over the stone and into pond below. Water lilies lined the edge of the pond near two of the granite boulders that were positioned at the water's edge under the dappled shade of river birches. A raised earthen platform was created behind rows of large, stacked canal stones, with irregular fragments arranged to mark entrance steps up to the platform that overlooks both the pond and the house.

After his wife's death in 2005, Fritz Neuenschwander listed the house for sale with local realtor "Bud" Byrne. Initially, there was interest in the house, but the steady deterioration and numerous unknowns in the cost of repair frightened many potential buyers. The location, on a busy state highway that was also near the flight path of airplanes during certain wind conditions, and the growing suburban sprawl of Columbus, made the location less desirable.

In 2008, several preservation-minded individuals became aware of the deteriorating condition of the house. An offer by a local developer to purchase the two-and-a-half-acre property for its demolition was an impetus for the preservationists and other local groups to attempt to draw attention to the property in hopes of finding a buyer interested in restoring the home. Kathy Mast Kane and Dave Vottero, two members of the Columbus Landmarks Foundation, produced a short video along with Preservation Ohio to coincide with the listing of Glenbrow on Preservation Ohio's 2009 Most Endangered List. That same year, two of Tony Smith's daughters, Kiki Smith and Seton Smith, both respected artists in their own right, visited the property with the desire to draw attention to it and attract a potential buyer. While the visit attracted media attention, resulting in an article in the local paper, it failed to find a buyer. Columbus Landmarks featured a twenty-eight-photograph tour of the home and later listed the property in its inaugural "Most Endangered List" in 2014. In their December 2013 newsletter, they also featured a lovely poem written about the property by a poet who had visited the abandoned ruin:

The Readability of Place; Blacklick, Ohio
by Rikki Santer

Steamy July morning to trespass
and bear witness to the junction
of three quarters of a century
and the Glenbrow Gunning House
where a miniature epic
slips slowly away.

How to abandon cedar, sandstone
and cypress to the stubborn
stubble of field and ravine
that beards over ghosts

of blueprint genius,
and domestic stride.

How to surrender the poetry
on two and a half acres—
a tennis court ragged
greens between its teeth,
swimming pool molasses
pregnant with cattails,
two vulture chicks stumbling
inside a stone tower.

Musty echoes of clinking
martinis and moonlit
soirees. Walls of drawers
pardon barren shoe boxes,
and dissolving sachets.
How much can a prairie
tiara sag with its beauty
still brave?

Squint beyond the warping
and cobwebbing. Kitchen
cabinets of butter, coral,
teal. Mathematical grids
of clerestory windows and
rainbowed light screens.
Stacked slabs of arenite
to cantilever the heart
of fireplace. A horizontal
vocabulary, the opened
body of home.

Jet planes and highway
traffic scar the memory
of this evaporating retreat
while spiders, mice
and dragonflies
keep the rhythm.

In 2009, Charles Birnbaum, an acclaimed landscape architect as well as founder and president of the Cultural Landscape Foundation (TCLF), also visited Glenbrow, taking photographs for his organization. "These special sites reveal aspects of our country's origins and development as well as our evolving relationships with the natural world," the TCLF website noted, emphasizing the importance of listed sites that promote and protect landscape heritage. The Gunning House was initially designated "At Risk" in the hopes of preserving it, with the following description: "This property illustrates the integral relationship between landscape and architecture that is the central tenant of organic architectural theory." They also listed the property under their 2009 Landslide section to draw attention to the unique features of the then threatened property. The Gunning House was also selected as an example of a Modernist Garden and Garden/Estate. Local preservationist Nathalie Wright observed that the Gunning House and its landscape "stands as an early example of mid-twentieth-century Organic-Modernist architecture in central Ohio." She added, "Like other organically inspired designs, particularly those designed utilizing Frank Lloyd Wright's philosophies, the Gunning House responds to and grows from its surroundings. The cultural landscape is an important component of the house, exemplified by how the site contributes to the house both as a historic designed landscape and as a largely intact, natural feature untouched by development."

The research made us aware that the property was special to many people who had visited the site over the years. The downside of all the attention paid to the deteriorating property was a steady stream of architecture enthusiasts, photographers, and, unfortunately, trespassing thieves, some with an interest in the architecture and others wanting to take a piece of history with them. Over the years, numerous photographers posted their photographs online, documenting the steady decay from both the elements and vandalism. Even by 2009, photographs show there were visual signs of a termite infestation off the kitchen and into the lounge, further scaring potential buyers.

One collection of photographs I discovered were from 2009 by an individual listed as "danchannel," which depicts the kitchen still intact, with appliances and no broken windows in the main house at the time. By chance, I scrolled through some additional photographs and recognized some people I knew from my work on voting rights issues. I contacted them and discovered the photographer was their son, a videographer who had founded a PBS affiliate, Ohio Channel, that provided Ohio statehouse coverage with locally produced programs. Dan and his wife, Heather, had once looked to purchase Glenbrow, but like so many others enamored by the charm, feared the unknown costs of restoration, especially without any previous building experience.

CHAPTER 7:
The Wait

As we awaited the court's decision, we were allowed to seal up broken windows and secure the house to prevent any further vandalism. We also decided to cut down the thick tangle of English ivy that crept up the four stories of the tower's textured stucco walls. We loaded up the car with plywood pieces, rolls of six mil thick plastic, a staple gun, and an axe. Joe brought a sketchbook and a marker to take notes.

The warm blue skies of late summer had now been replaced by cold bitter winds and the overcast gray of November. As we entered the property, we were surprised to find a car parked in the driveway. Two of our friends, John and Sara, both architects, had come to look at the house we planned to restore. Joe was on an architectural review board with John and had mentioned to him that we planned to visit the property to seal up the site for winter.

Northern winds had blown the remaining leaves off their branches and they swirled around as they collected at the edges of the carport and studio. The verdant charm and brightly colored crocuses had all faded, leaving an omnipresent gray. The property seemed much smaller without the foliage, as houses now appeared beyond the tennis court and across the ravine, while cars racing down Broad Street could be viewed between the trunks of the denuded tree line.

John and Sara, cloaked in their cold weather wear, were standing in the windswept tall grasses near the pond's edge. The vantage point provided them with a clear view of the carport, the partially collapsed walkway, and the attached main house. I could tell from their concerned faces that they had some doubts about the task that lay ahead of us. "If you had seen it a couple months earlier, you would better understand how the site won us over," I replied, starting to have some doubts of my own!

Inside, the house did not appear much better. The soothing views of dappled sunlight filtering through the verdant ravine were now replaced with gray, denuded tree trunks veining their way up toward the overcast sky. The house, dark and musty, was still in disarray, with fallen ceiling panels, cellulose insulation, and broken glass scattered about. The jewel-toned kitchen cabinets remained pulled away from the walls by copper scavengers and were dulled by years of accumulated dust and grime.

"The architects were really young and inexperienced, so there are several design flaws that will need to be rectified," Joe explained. Pointing upward in the kitchen, he said, "The clerestory windows sit at the same elevation as the roof, without proper flashing beneath them. Years of snow build-up, which would melt because of the warmth of the uninsulated house caused the melted snow that's become flowing water to travel down through and beneath the window frames and settle in the roof rafters and the ceiling's plywood panels. The water caused the roof structure to rot and created the perfect environment for insects as well." Joe pointed out the obvious termite destruction to the wall and frame of the built-in sofa around the corner from the kitchen. Our structural engineer had assessed this and was sure that more of the structure would need to be rebuilt. "Check this out! Instead of two-by-twelve rafters, there are three stacked two-by-fours. This was a technique of Wright's to lower cost at a time when labor was cheap at the end of the Depression. It must have been less expensive to stack three two-by-fours than to use a single two-by-twelve!" Joe explained. "Wright also liked to cascade the heights of the exterior soffits as they extended outward from the walls, which made the roof plane appear extremely thin, so I suspect the stacking technique made that process easier in the days of hand tools."

Joe explained how we would remove the ceiling panels, assess the roof framing, and replace the rest of the roof assembly. "The big job will be to remove the concrete floor slab and replace the hydronic heating system that Wright referred to as gravity heat." Pointing to the floor's burnt orange-red concrete with its two-foot-by-four-foot grid pattern, he said, "This house looks like a Wright Usonian," a reference to Wright's mid-century open floor-plan homes that utilized his principles of organic architecture at a modest price point. "They had worked on Wright's Suntop homes and had just finished Wright's Armstrong house in Indiana, which utilizes a thirty-sixty-ninety-degree shift in geometry, but the shift is between the separate floors. This house uses the topography of the ravine with the same angles on its single floor as it snakes along the edge."

After they left, we went to work attaching plywood over openings in the main house and made sure the doors were secured to prevent trespassing. We then turned to the tower where Joe and Fia installed pieces of the six mil plastic over broken windows while Maren and I used an axe to chop the bases of the thick ivy growing up the sides of the tower. At times, both of us would pull loose a branch of vine in a tug of war with the tall structure. We locked the door to the tower with a padlock and posted new "No Trespassing" signs on the doors of the tower and the carport storeroom, which would be visible to drivers who pulled into the property. We placed several concrete blocks along the driveway before the tree line with another "No Trespassing" sign attached. This would prevent people from driving into the property and hopefully avert any additional damage or thievery.

Continuing my research on the house and the young designers, I also explored whether there were any surviving family members who had grown up at Glenbrow. Rob and Mary had four children, all of whom were raised there, and I hoped to reach out to them in order to discover more information. By chance, I came upon an archived article from January 1962 about the Gunning's eldest daughter, Nora, who had been involved in a terrible automobile accident near Nashville. Nineteen at the time of the crash, Nora had survived the harrowing incident, which resulted in thirty broken bones and a collapsed lung, and which had left her in a coma for several weeks—a testament to her strong will and fighting spirit that I would later encounter. Nora is a writer whose publications range from poetry to allegories to advocacy for civil rights and people with disabilities to trade publications.

Tom Gunning was a professor emeritus of cinema and media studies at the University of Chicago and a recipient of a 1998 Guggenheim Fellowship in Film, Video, and Radio Studies. Tom had published approximately one hundred publications concentrating on early cinema, American avant-garde cinema, and the culture of modernity from which cinema arose. One of his latest books, coauthored with several colleagues, *Fantasia of Color in Early Cinema,* had a foreword by Martin Scorsese.

Grace Gunning is an artist residing in upstate New York who creates beautiful reliquary boxes, many from found objects, with the aid of antique machines and tools from the late 1800s and early 1900s. Each metal piece is unique, often centered on the themes of nature or mystical allegories. Besides her special reliquary boxes, she also creates jewelry and whimsical table lamps using metal that incorporates iconic images as well as nature scenes. Grace was the first family member I made contact with via email, having discovered her contact information on a website for her art. She was thrilled to hear of our plans for restoration. She wrote, "We had said our goodbyes to our beloved home and had thought our home would return to nature from where the inspiration first arose."

Seth Gunning was the youngest of the children and, like his siblings, very creative. He had a passion for translating the classics with a particular fondness for Plato. His studies took him to New York University and the East Village, where he became a member of Mofungo, a no-wave band influenced by jazz and English punk bands, which formed in the late 1970s out of an NYU dorm room. Seth is featured as a keyboardist playing organ and synthesizer on their 1981 album, *End of the World,* and *El Salvador* from 1982.

During my research, I also discovered an online community of Frank Lloyd Wright enthusiasts had also discussed the property, providing details and descriptions from their visits to the property in previous years.

There was a regular cast of contributors—many architects, some Wright homeowners, and others with experience in restoration—and all of them were very knowledgeable about Wright's principles, architecture, and the important place Wright held in the history of American architecture. Although some of the commenters thought the house was rather primitive, most were very positive:

> This is a wonderful site and a fine early house to study the deep meaning of FLW's organic architectural ideas outside the realm of his personal influence.

> The interior spaces look remarkably sophisticated for 1940, a little like John Lautner nine years later, it seems like a so. cal or desert house placed in Ohio. even though the stone work has a primitive quality, this is not a rustic cabin, but an imaginative piece of organic architecture.

> The two-story studios (?) is sort of Schindler? Who was the architect? The house comes closer to Usonian than anything else I've seen at Rush Creek And so cool! The narrow stacked horizontal windows are unique, while the long thin strip windows and the flush glazing on the opposite wall are somehow like what one might find in a later and more metallic architecture—very "now," in fact. But the woodsy and wild environment, both built and natural, that exists today is strikingly Organic, in every sense. Interior details are, again, somewhat Schindlerian, to my eye—specifically the built-in cabinetry. The masonry, on the other hand is yet another take on Wright's signature stonework, and one of the more successful ones from what I see.

> It also speaks of another important fact: the influence of FLW

and organic architecture was an intellectual wildfire that instilled significant energy into a generation of young people before and after WWII.

Of all the non-Wright buildings in peril that have been shown on this site, Gunning is the best by far.

Since the property was not yet in our hands and I didn't want to jinx our chances or draw attention that might lead to a possible bidding war, I lurked without commenting that we were under contract on the house. I did, however, privately contact one of the contributors, David, who had posted photographs of his visit to the property several years earlier. He had the photographs on a file sharing website that was about to shut down and I wanted to ensure that his photographs would not disappear along with the website. I explained that we were under contract and awaiting a court decision. David was thrilled. He provided me access to his photographs from 2009 and actually later visited with his wife while we were restoring the property.

I also contacted the preservation architect who had appeared in the Preservation Ohio video that I discovered online. Dave Vottero was the Director of Design at Schooley Caldwell Associates, a highly regarded local firm that specialized in preservation, a position once held by Joe. Dave had worked on the revival of Frank Lloyd Wright's Westcott House, a 1908 Prairie Style house that had been in a terrible ruinous condition prior to its restoration. He was thrilled with our intentions and offered to provide us with files that included house floor plans, elevations, and historic photographs. I informed him that I would be very interested once the sale was completed as I didn't want to jinx our chances. Dave also let us know, "I prepared a study adding two more homes to the site in hopes of making the purchase more cost effective." He was happy when I thanked him, but that we intended to keep the property as is and just focus on restoring the existing buildings.

CHAPTER 8:
Finally, It's Ours!

In late spring of 2014, we finally heard the good news we were hoping for—the court had agreed to a settlement. We told Elaine that we wanted to close as soon as possible. After so many months of anticipation and fear that we might lose the property to developers who were interested in razing the buildings for commercial land, we were finally ready to start work on a project that would change the course of our lives.

One of the first people I contacted was Dave Vottero, the preservation architect who had offered us files on the house. He was ecstatic with our news and provided us with a trove of information containing floor plans, drawings, and historic photographs.

The date that was set in early June was shortly after our older daughter's high school graduation and unknowingly, we had scheduled a party in her honor the day after the closing. My brother, Doug, and a friend were coming into town for the weekend, so after so much anticipation, our initial restoration work would be slightly delayed. The day following the party, we drove out with them to show off our future home. It was a beautiful sunny day in early June, and the first thing that caught my brother's eye was the looming tower, no longer enveloped in vines.

"Wow, that's cool! Let's check that out!" Doug replied upon seeing the four-story tower built into the hillside. "It's really nasty inside. We need to get it mold remediated," I told him, but he was as intent to tour it as our daughter Maren was to show it off. Joe opened the weathered screen door, unlocked the padlock that we had placed on it the previous November, and we stepped inside the damp musty entrance. The slate floor was covered in leaves and other organic debris from years of neglect. The room was accented by overhead beams that lined the surface of the low ceiling, which drew your eye to the windows. The verdant foliage filtered the sunlight shining through years of cobwebs along the window frames, leaving the room dark. The vertical windows protruded out to mitered glass corners that created an uninterrupted vista of the wooded ravine. Squares of colored glass in red, green, and yellow formed a prism on the large desk in the center of the room. Stacks of drawers reached up from the floor to the waist-high window ledge. To the right of the desk was a trifold full-length mirror, behind which was moldy drywall, saturated by a recent rain. "There is extensive water damage in here, especially in that corner of the building," Joe explained, seeing my brother's expression as he peered in that direction.

The interest in the building was soon interrupted by unearthly screeches coming from upstairs that were like nothing we had ever heard before. "What the heck was that?" Doug asked. "I don't know but I'm not about to find out!" I replied back as we all headed for the exit. "Sounds like a dying alien!" Fia added.

Outside, Doug scanned the debris in the carport and picked up a broken handle from an old shovel. "Who's with me?" he asked. Fia, his friend Jan, and I decided to stay back as Joe and Maren volunteered to accompany Doug in search of the source of the cacophony residing somewhere in the floors above.

I could hear their heavy footsteps slowly make their way up the stairwell along with the muffled sound of their strategizing. "It's two large bird chicks just inside the door to the roof terrace," Joe informed us. Then I heard groans from my brother, Joe, and Maren as they rushed down the stairs, gagging as they exited through the door with their hands covering their noses and mouths. The chicks had regurgitated a foul-smelling substance upon seeing the interlopers approach their nest. After several minutes of recovery in the fresh air, the trio wrapped sweatshirts over their faces and reentered the tower to coax the chicks out to the roof.

The chicks were almost ten inches tall with pointed beaks, and they sat on the landing just inside the doorway to the rooftop terrace. The door was partially open, so using an old broom, along with the shovel handle, Doug and Joe coaxed the birds outside onto the roof. We soon learned that the chicks were turkey vultures, and the smell was a defense mechanism of vomiting semidigested carrion—the meat of dead animals that vultures eat, fed to them by their mother. The tower was then secured for remediation.

CHAPTER 9:
The Restoration

Although this was the fifth house that we were about to restore, as I look back, I don't think either of us fully understood the enormity of the task that laid ahead of us. This was probably a good thing. The months of wait, coupled with the discovery of the house's history, provided us with the motivation to delve right in. The first goal was to fully assess the structure's integrity so that a game plan and the necessary construction drawings could be completed.

With Joe working full time, Maren and I were tasked with clearing brush to create paths to the house. We purchased a commercial bushwhacker that used a blade to cut through the tall thistle and small saplings so that we could eventually mow the yard with our newly acquired lawn tractor. We cut down the vines and hauled away broken branches that blocked the pathways. Half of the original roof was shrouded in encroaching vines, so we clipped away the edges, depositing the debris down the ravine. We shoveled inches of composted soil off the roof, pulling saplings and tall weeds that had rooted in the organic material.

Years of neglect had left the surrounding trees shrouded in thick vines, usually grapevine and English ivy, but sometimes the hairy vines of noxious poison ivy. Maren and I worked on its removal throughout the entire summer on days too glorious to be trapped inside, surrounded by the dust of deconstruction. The vine removal on the trees that were in groves along the roadside and tennis court were a breeze compared to the difficult terrain of the steep hillside!

Once this grueling chore was completed, we realized that there were a half dozen mature ash trees near the house that were dead as a result of the emerald ash borers that were decimating ash trees across the country. An arborist came out and determined that we needed to cut down six mature dead ash trees that were dangerously close to the house, an added expense we never anticipated. Since the trees were on the steep hillside, they would be dropped with only the smaller branches hauled away. The thick trunks were left on the slope, providing shelter for wildlife while slowly decomposing into the soil. They also examined the two mature black locusts in front of the house on the raised lawn, removing dead branches and securing them with cabling for safety in high winds. They also suggested that we remove smaller healthy ash trees. "Eventually, they will all die from the infestation and treating them would cost about $150 per tree per year. It's not worth it," I was told.

Since the house was going to remain unoccupied for some time during construction, insurance agencies were reluctant to provide coverage. We eventually found a carrier, but coverage required the stipulation that the covered walkway be immediately removed, as it was badly deteriorated, and they deemed it a hazard. In deconstructing the walkway, we discovered extensive damage from carpenter ants in the wood supports connected to the stuccoed piers and extending far into the roof structure of the storage room areas of the carport. Joe determined that this area would need to be rebuilt, but our first priority was not the carport roof, but the work of roof restructuring, roof replacement and the closing-in of the main house before winter set in.

Several times, we had met with a contractor about building the new house on our split Bexley lot, but Joe had difficulty in reaching him. We soon discovered that he had moved out of town after an unfavorable health diagnosis. Until Joe could hire a new contractor, we would begin the process of deconstruction to determine the extent of the damage and continue to develop our plans for the restoration.

Maren pleaded with us to allow her to work on the house instead of returning to a lifeguard job she had previously held and that she had recruited several of her friends from swim team to help as a summer job. "Pleeease! It will be great experience that I may never get again. Lifeguarding is so boring!" She was planning to leave in the fall to begin architecture school. Unlike her sister, Sofia, Maren had no qualms about dirty work or hard labor. Several of her friends, planning to study engineering and industrial design, convinced their parents as well.

They donned Tyvek suits, masks, and hardhats, and armed with crowbars and hammers, they began to remove the two-by-four Douglas fir plywood ceiling panels. While removing branches from the tennis court one day, Maren and her friend Zach, covered in dust and their N-95 masks, gray with a coating of grime, came to show me their latest discovery. "Look what we found in the cellulose insulation!" she said, pointing toward her friend. Zach extended his filthy, thick, suede work gloves to reveal a snakeskin over two feet long. "Yikes! Any living things up there?" I asked, taking a step back. "No living snakes. It's probably too hot for them to be up in the ceiling," Maren explained. "This is so cool!" Zach commented as he maneuvered the skin, examining it from different angles. "You don't want to see what else we found—mouse skeletons!" warned Maren, knowing of my irrational fear of rodents. "You got that right!"

We devised an alpha-numeric grid system, marking the back of each panel so that it could be returned to its previous location after restoration, temporarily stacking the panels under the soffit outside the front door. When Joe returned from work, he would evaluate the pieces and determine which were salvable, which were partially salvable, and which were condemned to the dumpster due to extensive damage. After a couple days of this routine, we determined it was not worth marking the panels since such a large quantity were in such bad shape from water damage, insects, or both, that many would require disposal.

Summer months in central Ohio are often marked with torrential downpours. After one heavy rain, in which two inches fell within a few hours, the patio outside the kitchen door flooded and the formerly walled upper lawn poured down a torrent, entering through the kitchen door, as had obviously happened in previous years. Fia and I donned our rain boots and shoveled the muddy water into buckets while Joe and Maren carried the buckets up behind the western bedroom and then emptied them to run down the ravine. Water was also leeching through the lower block retaining walls of the partially buried western bedroom. Joe hired an excavator, who dug trenches to circumnavigate the entire front and end of the house and patio, adding drainage lines and trench drains that would allow the water to flow into the ravine. A separate second drainage system was also added around the partially below-grade wall of the western bedroom that was excavated and sealed with a polymeric waterproofing and backfilled with gravel.

During that first summer, our breaks were often spent exploring our new landscape, most of which was down the steep wooded slope and along the creek. Having downed the dead ashes and cleared many of the vines that had blocked the view of the water, we now had a better prospect of the beautiful terrain. The creek had a bedrock bottom, and the sides were lined with stone, hence the water was crystal clear. Shaded by mature trees, the temperature was ten degrees cooler down there, which was welcome relief after the dirty, hot work inside. We would sit on the stones, take our boots off, and wade in the cool water. Most days, the water flowed like a babbling brook, the stone formations creating swirling eddies and small waterfalls. The trickle of the water, coupled with the filtered sunlight and cooler temperatures, made it the ideal break location. The faint sounds of songbirds were barely audible over the moving water, but the cacophony of traffic noise from Broad Street above us was completely erased. Sometimes, we rearranged stones to redirect the flow in order to increase the intensity of water over a fall and generate an additional rush sound. We also enjoyed examining the stone for fossils and unusual shapes, stacking pieces we wanted to bring uphill for display. Traveling up the banks, we discovered the creek had a confluence a couple hundred feet upstream, past a natural level change in bedrock that created a small waterfall. In the other direction, extensive erosion had left stratified cliffs. Although wading in the cool water was a peaceful adventure, the slow meandering trickle could quickly change to whitewater rapids after a heavy rain, reminding us that the power of water can be threatening as well as soothing.

By mid-August, the dog days of summer had settled in, and although the house, shaded by large trees, remained cool, outdoor work was stifling. Maren left for her first year of college and school resumed for many of our other helpers. While Joe was interviewing contractors, I was left to handle one-person tasks, focusing on the removal of invasive plants and attempting to resurrect the previous gardens that were buried beneath. While weeding in the sunken garden that bordered the carport, walkway, and eastern bedroom, I discovered a serpentine stone retaining wall, encircling a courtyard that was covered in dense honeysuckle, bramble, and poison ivy. Armed with long sleeves and over-the-elbow rubber gloves, I attempted to remove the noxious plants, but by the following day, my arms were covered in itchy welts. I thought at first I must have been bitten by some insect, but as the rash grew, along with a more intense itch, I soon discovered that it was due to poison ivy. I was unaware that rubber allowed the oily toxin to penetrate through the material. The rash was so extensive that it required a trip to the emergency room, and I was forced to wear long sleeves to cover the scarring for the rest of the season, even after my treatment.

Although it was another unanticipated expense, I had several landscapers come out to give quotes for the removal of the extensive poison ivy that was growing around the property. Seeing the extent of the thick vines, none of them were interested in bidding. I discovered that goats would eat the ivy, but that the roots would remain, leaving it an ongoing problem, as the plants would reemerge. Worried that our dogs would continually bring it inside, I knew I would have to eradicate it by pulling it all out by the roots. It led me to research the effects of the toxin, so from that point forward, I wore Tyvek suits, masks, and nitrile shoulder-length chemical resistant gloves and waited until after a decent rain, so I could easily pull the plant, roots and all, from the ground. "I'm probably on some homeland security watch list," I would joke, "from ordering large quantities of Tyvek suits and chemical resistant gloves!"

After recovering from the poison ivy, I resumed work in the sunken courtyard. Using a dandelion tool to remove some deep-rooted weeds, I hit something solid. Further digging revealed a limestone patio on the side and back off the eastern, future main bedroom that had been covered by years of composted vegetation. "Buried treasure," I said as I pointed out my discovery to Joe. With two large boulders situated slightly off center, and surrounded by the curvilinear stone retaining wall, I decided that I would create a zen garden that would not only be visible from along the walkway, but would also create the perfect view from a soaking tub in our future bathroom. First, however, a lot more weeding was required.

We started the restoration at the tail end of the Great Recession, and by our June 2014 closing, the repressed demand for tradesmen, many of which left their trades out of frustration, caused a tight labor market. We discovered long queues in the various trades to provide their services. There was so much demand that some trades had the benefit of choosing easy projects over complicated work such as our restoration.

By the end of August, we hired a contractor and work began to proceed quickly. The goal was to finish deconstruction and to replace compromised structural elements so that a new roof could be in place before the first snowfall. The carpenters finished dismantling the plywood wall and ceiling panels, rebuilding sections of walls and roof framing where the compromised structure was badly deteriorated. The entire roof deck was removed. When the props were removed from below the roof of the future main bedroom, the roof collapsed, which deposited years of tar and gravel from numerous past reroofing jobs into the room. It was during this phase that our good friends, the Kurras, first visited our new property. I could see the look of shock in their expressions. "I know it looks bad now, but the site has so much potential," I told them. It was clear that others, including me sometimes, had a hard time visualizing the end result.

All the original doors and windows were removed for restoration and to retrofit the original single-plane glass with energy efficient, low-E, insulating glass. Exceptions included the inoperable upper clerestory kitchen windows that Joe wanted to be operable for ventilation purposes, and the kitchen door that had suffered from many years of water penetration. Joe suggested the upper clerestory windows were not worth saving because he didn't see a place for them, but I stuck them inside the tower just in case.

Joe drew up plans and met with the contractor almost daily before and after work to ensure the job was proceeding correctly. The contractor was both a civil engineer and a licensed contractor, but despite coming with good recommendations, Joe soon discovered puzzled looks and a need to explain too many things in depth, which led him to question the contractor's ability to comprehend the detail drawings in Joe's construction documents. Since the project had so many unknowns and Joe wanted it built correctly, instead of the fastest and easiest way possible, he had suggested a time and materials basis, instead of a lump-sum bid, for the job. We soon realized we were paying for mistakes, including the partial removal of them and rebuilding the corrections. And with the contractor's percentage on top of it all! "We've got to get a new roof on before it snows or we are screwed, and it is almost impossible in this economy to find another contractor," Joe would argue when I suggested firing him. "I can't do this work alone with my job. It takes at least two strong men to lift twenty-foot-long two-by-twelves into place." We both knew from experience that the construction process was stressful. This added friction increased the stress level significantly!

In one of the errors, the kitchen-counter-level windows were ordered incorrectly and we were forced to eat the cost. After that, Joe decided to oversee the ordering of all the new windows, doors, and replacement glass. Again, instead of disposing of the errors, I stashed them in the tower, awaiting an opportunity to create a use for them in the future.

The original house had French doors on the ravine side of the house, lining both the "Point Room" and the room adjacent to the kitchen called the "Lounge" on the original floor plan. During the 1964 addition, Ted van Fossen moved a pair of French doors that were located there into the new western bedroom, replacing them with a single piece of glass. We decided to relocate a pair of French doors from an irregularly shaped area between the living room and future main bedroom that had originally been a breezeway to the carport. This move allowed for a continuous line of French doors along the ravine. A new pair of French doors and matching fixed windows were purchased for the ravine side of this space that connected the living room to what would become our main bedroom. Joe ordered eight, large, six-and-a-half-foot-tall casement windows for the future bedroom to match the new window in the area of the former breezeway, ensuring the adjacent areas would be consistent. "This eastern end of the house will then have a consistent appearance to its fenestration" said Joe, using an architect's term for windows.

New, energy efficient replacement skylights were ordered, and two more would be added—one for just inside the entrance and one in front of the fireplace near the horizontal stacked windows to diminish the need for artificial lighting during the day. In the raised section of the kitchen and the Point Room bath, ten operable clerestory windows were ordered to provide natural ventilation for these spaces. Both the kitchen and the laundry room would also receive new exterior glass doors. During deconstruction, it was revealed that there must have been a door, removed at some point to add an air-conditioning unit, outside the kitchen patio. With no need for a door in that location, a large casement window was placed to add more source of daylight and ventilation, while limiting expenses in a project rapidly going over budget.

The window and door restoration included ten pairs of original French doors, thirty-two horizontal windows approximately one foot by four foot, six horizontal, nine-inch-by-twenty-two-inch windows for behind the kitchen counters, and four casement windows—all removed, lightly sanded, and retrofitted with energy efficient glass panes. In replacing the broken mitered glass for the ravine corner window, we discovered that double-pane, mullion-less corner glazing would cost about seven thousand dollars, so we opted for single pane—still over eleven hundred dollars installed.

One of the house's original design flaws was in the placement of the upper kitchen clerestory windows at the same elevation as the roof, with subsequent roof repairs actually placing the bottom of the window glass below the level of the roof. The new kitchen roof would be rebuilt twelve inches higher to allow for proper flashing below the bottoms of the clerestories. The prominent stone wall along the front entrance would have its crumbling stone along several top courses rebuilt, with the new kitchen roof cantilevering beyond it so it would not deteriorate in the future.

Several stonemasons the contractor had used in the past were booked up for several months into the future. When Adam, the head carpenter, suggested a young mason who was just starting out who was available, we were willing to interview him for the job.

AJ, the young stonemason, had trained under his father but had recently decided to go out on his own. He came out in his black pickup truck and was thrilled about the possibility of working on a project where he could show off his craftsmanship. The first priority was to rebuild the kitchen stone wall and to bring the stone fireplace chimney up to code so that the roof framing could begin. We decided to hire him one project at a time to evaluate his work.

AJ's team consisted of himself and two other young men in their mid- to late-twenties. Rough around the edges but polite in the rural tradition, the guys were unbelievably strong from working at their daily craft.

There was a need to replace deteriorated stone as well as for the additional projects, with a wealth of stone along the creek below. AJ and his posse, as Adam had nicknamed his workers, descended down to the creek, compiling a large pile near the water's edge. Despite the August heat, the bedrock creek was about ten degrees cooler and heavily shaded by the mature trees. It seemed like a good time to retrieve stone from along the banks. Soon the guys started carrying the rocks up the steep incline to the house. After a few trips, AJ came up to me and said, "Man, that's a steep hill. I'm going to hire some young bucks to carry the stone up the hill." I laughed, "You guys are young bucks! Now I don't feel so bad about my failed attempts."

The next day, the posse arrived with two young guys who looked as if they might be linemen for a high school football team. They descended down the hillside and began the daunting task of transporting the stone up the steep hill. After a short period, AJ found me wrestling with grapevine that was tangled in the row of spruce trees and told me, "Well, that didn't work. They didn't even last two hours before they quit. We need a plan B." AJ and the posse left to search local stone yards in the area. After some time, they returned in a commercial dump truck filled with stone. "I found this pile in the corner of a stone yard nearby, covered in vines, that matches your stone. I bought the whole pile so we will have enough for the future." Then they set about unloading their heavy cargo, weathered by the elements to a near perfect match, and created a stone yard just beyond the western bedroom. "We have our own stone yard, just like the Gothic cathedrals had!" Joe exclaimed upon seeing it.

The head carpenter, Adam, became a regular fixture at Glenbrow. A skilled finish carpenter, framing was beneath his skill expertise, but he loved taking pride in his work almost as much as he loved the wooded setting. "Man, I don't think I can ever go back to finishing a renovation of some tract home or working in a windowless shop after this." Arriving earlier each day to the site than me, he would inform me of his daily animal sitings. "There was a coyote traveling along the creek this morning," or, "That's a red-tailed hawk nesting in that sycamore tree along the creek," would start my workday. I soon could distinguish the different birds overhead by their sounds, or what animals had visited the site by their scat.

Although Joe and Adam seemed like polar opposites, both shared a devotion to quality workmanship and respect for the project, which led to a friendship. Adam was slightly younger than me, with a close-cut military crew cut. Although he was only slighter taller than me, he was perhaps one of the strongest men I ever witnessed. He would carry the old, waterlogged plywood panels above his head to the dumpster, pieces Maren and I together would struggle to carry. The downside to Adam was that he listened to sports radio, something I had never had to encounter before. Who knew there was a market for three straight hours of talking about Tom Brady? I knew practically nothing about Tom Brady before we started the project but came to despise his very existence by the end of it. Luckily, when Joe worked with Adam, he would listen to a classic rock station and the two of them would belt out the words on every song. "They play the same songs over and over on that classic rock station," Joe would sometimes complain. "Don't you dare complain!" I would tell him, "I get Tom fricking Brady, all day long, every fricking day!"

The framing was getting nearer to completion as the dry weather of September approached, making us confident that the roof would be on before the first snow arrived. Then, in a blink of an eye, the workers stopped coming to the site. After the second day, Joe called, and the contractor told him he had a project that needed immediate attention. Several more days passed with no work and Joe became frantic, reminding the contractor that winter was fast approaching and there was still a lot of work to be done. We were told that he would find some replacement people. He hired a friend's son who arrived without tools (or skills, for that matter!), and Adam returned part-time to train him. Adam was obviously not pleased with the training, so after finding a coiled black snake in the western bedroom, he sent the young guy in there to finish something while he ran an errand. The following day, when I returned to the site, Kevin had completely swept out and organized the carport woodpile in order to avoid the house. Two more workers also appeared—one out of retirement who I feared might keel over at any time and another who came for a few days and disappeared. We learned from Adam that he had been arrested for failing to pay child support.

There was increasing tension whenever the contractor was on site with Adam, and then on one Saturday, Joe received a phone call from Adam. Adam had discovered that he was being paid about the same amount as the young guy without tools or skills, causing him to promptly quit working for our contractor. He also told us that the team had been pulled off the job because the contractor wanted work done on his own house. Joe expressed his disappointment that Adam was leaving the job. "If you need help after the roof was on give me a call. I enjoy working on this project but I'm not working for him anymore."

Joe and I were going to the work site when he had time during the week and all day during the weekends, in a race with the weather. The two-week halt in work, followed by the underwhelming part-time effort, had set us behind schedule.

Then came the snow. On November 17, 2014, several inches of wet snow fell, and the forecast going forward was calling for freezing temperatures. At this point, only raw oriented strand board (OSB) sheathing covered the flat roof. Joe came home from work early and went out to the site to make sure the workers knew how urgent it was to clear the roof to protect the exposed sheathing and prevent ice from forming, which would have to be chopped away, potentially damaging the sheathing. Fia accompanied him, since school had been cancelled, wanting to photograph the snow for her studio art class.

When they returned after several hours, Fia was quick to show me her photographs, including those of Joe shoveling the roof by himself. There he was atop a sheathed flat roof, cantilevering over a steep wooded ravine as heavy snow fell and the wind howled around him. Despite the picturesque scene I was beyond livid!

My husband is a hands-on guy when it comes to construction, but just five years earlier, he had suffered a major accident. A fall left him with an incomplete spinal cord injury of the third through fifth segments of his cervical spine as well as a brain bleed. After two seven-hour surgeries that attached plates to the anterior and posterior cervical spine, he spent months in rehabilitation, relearning simple functions and how to walk again. He had also gone through an intense Christopher and Dana Reeve Foundation program focusing on his balance and gait. His improvement was so remarkable for the type of injury that he had recovered from that he later participated in studies with the foundation.

The contractor responsible for the project knew of Joe's medical history, yet he had pulled his workers during good weather to work on improvements on his own house and was nowhere in sight when snow fell on the unprotected sheathing. The task of shoveling the snow off a flat roof that cantilevered off a steep hill was left to my sixty-five-year-old husband with balance issues. My blood was boiling!

When I confronted the contractor, he said he was attempting to save us money by not bringing workers out on a day when they would not be fully productive. "Fire his sorry ass!" I screamed. Joe reminded me there was no one else to complete the roof and promised me that as soon as the roof was on, the contractor would be gone forever.

A week after, with improving weather, the roofers were onsite, installing the tapered insulation in an arrangement Joe devised to drain two thirds of the rainwater toward the ravine and one third to the front. The EPDM white membrane was installed shortly afterward. Two galvanized half-round gutters were added—one above the French doors of our future dining room and the other above the kitchen patio, since the exterior concrete of neither of them possessed even the slightest slope necessary to drain water from the roof away from the house. The gutters would also prevent rainwater from splashing the glass below. In both cases, the water would spout out to an artfully placed collection of river rocks below, before draining down the ravine.

Outside, the stonemasons began to build a concrete block retaining wall along the kitchen patio with a linear drain opening below. In their excavation, they discovered a heavy, rusted object about six inches in height. What was this object? Knowing that Tony Smith's family owned a foundry, I contacted his estate to see if perhaps the piece was an early prototype for his monumental sculptures to come. Although its form was rounded, I had seen his paintings in the 1950s adopt similar shapes. Unfortunately, a post inquiring about it on Facebook revealed it to be an old tooth from the excavation equipment used on the original house construction—unfortunately, not an early and very valuable Tony Smith sculpture.

After replacing the washed-out wall outside the kitchen with a concrete block retaining wall so that no collapses would occur in the future, a stone veneer would be added to match nearby walls. This would ensure that no further erosion would jeopardize the house during future deluges.

The masons then turned to rebuilding the cantilevering planter outside the Point Room that was in unstable condition. They also created a new planter at the edge of the rear patio where the concrete had badly deteriorated, outside what would become our dining room. Instead of patching the deteriorated areas of the patio outside the French doors, we had them remove the entire two-foot-wide strip and build a planter on top of the concrete block foundation wall that was similar to the Point Room's, though it emerged from the ground at the top of the slope. "We can grow shade plants in the new planter, and it will define the drop off edge without a need for a railing," Joe explained.

By Christmas of 2014, the roof was on and the house was closed in, with pieces of plywood over openings in anticipation of the restored and/or new windows and doors that had been ordered. With plywood covering the window openings, the lack of daylight, coupled with the newly completed roof, made the interior seem dark and foreboding. Work lights provided subtle relief, but there was little for me to do inside until spring arrived.

CHAPTER 10:
Diamond in the Rough

2015 was Glenbrow's seventy-fifth anniversary—its diamond anniversary. As the year began, our concrete contractors removed the original gridded concrete floor, leaving six inches around the periphery. This would not disturb the foundations or the exterior walls, which were attached to the slab by the original embedded anchor bolts. The brutal cold of January set in, with just a fireplace and construction salamanders (portable heat sources) to heat the interior workspace. The men jackhammered and removed the broken slabs of old concrete, deteriorated iron, and copper pipes from the long defunct radiant heat systems, wheeling them up the temporary wooden ramp they had built to the more accessible ground level for future removal. When we first purchased the property, I had initially hoped there might be some way to thread new functional heat tubing through the existing system to prevent the need to remove the concrete floor, but after seeing the condition of the pipes, I was glad for Joe's insistence to "do the job right."

With little to do until warmer weather arrived, Joe worked to finish drawings of the future configuration of spaces along with the numerous finish details for the house. We decided the western bedroom would be shortened by four feet to allow more space in the former "lounge" that we would use as a dining room. The bath portion of that bedroom was reconfigured to move plumbing supply lines off the exterior outside wall. This move, when coupled with the fact that it would no longer need its own water heater, would allow the stone shower to double in size.

For the original enclosed carport that was to become an open-space main bedroom suite, Joe drew up plans that would maintain unimpeded views by eliminating the walls between the bathroom and bedroom. We enjoyed the peaceful landscape over privacy and elected to keep the room as open as possible. The bed would face the tall windows along the ravine, providing us a vista that included winter sunrises as well as the changing seasons. A wall jogged from behind the headboard and ended at the shower, with an opening to divide the sleeping and bath area from a walk-in closet and laundry room. To ensure privacy from the rest of the house, yet allow spatial flexibility, full-height pocket doors would be used in both the main bedroom suite and western bedroom, instead of the previous accordion doors.

During the winter months, I had the property annexed into an adjacent suburb in order to tap into city water. The well would be maintained to use for landscaping. We had heard that local well failures were occurring, and we didn't want to take any chances supplying the entire house. We discovered that the sanitary sewer line was across multiple lanes of recently expanded Broad Street and would potentially cost up to six figures to access, so we decided to keep the existing septic system, which had been replaced less than a decade before.

March arrived, along with warmer temperatures and the windows Joe had ordered. Maren's spring break was spent helping Joe install the new operable clerestory windows around the raised roof of the kitchen. Adam returned to work full time, functioning as a project manager overseeing the daily work. Gone was his crew cut, and in its place was long hair and a goatee. The working environment became more relaxed. "Dude, this site is rubbing off on you!" we joked.

The board-and-batten cypress siding was removed, marked, lightly sanded, and then stained with two coats of a protective stain that matched both the color of the weathered boards as well as the color of the new factory-coated window frames. We chose the stain over clear coat applications after discovering the process would need to be repeated every few years, a chore we did not want to face as we approached retirement. After staining, Joe and Adam would reinstall the siding with new square drive screws to replace the old slot head screws, which are difficult to use with a power drill. We learned that in 1940, they were the only screw type that existed. There was only the need to purchase one new siding board on the entire house—a testament to the durability of old growth cypress.

The strength of the economy made it difficult to find a plumber who was willing to take on the task of installing new water and gas lines from the street, plumbing the entire house, and installing the complicated hydronic heat system. We finally found a commercial plumbing contractor, but just as they were getting to full speed, they won a huge fulfillment center contract and placed our project on the back burner. We could not proceed on the main house until their work was completed.

With no choice but to wait on the plumbers, the focus turned to rebuilding the studio, carport, and the walkway that attached to the main house. Maren and several of her friends rotated through, serving as Adam's assistants. Although the walkway roof had already been removed, there were still old roof beams connecting several of the stuccoed piers to the studio. It was apparent that two of the piers, plus the majority of the studio walls, were rotting and infested with carpenter ants and would need to be demolished. Once the support beams were removed, the heavy piers became dangerous. "I have an idea," Adam said. "We'll attach a rope, pull them down, and drag them away with my truck." We attached heavy cable to the four-foot-wide piers and Adam slowly pulled the massive pieces down and then deposited them near the dumpster. Maren and her friend Zach took turns with sledgehammers, further breaking up the piers, reducing them to chunks of stucco and metal lath along with the deteriorated wood that were of manageable size for placing in the dumpster.

When he was pulling down one of the studio walls, Adam found two gold necklaces in between the walls of the "Monk's Cell." "I finally found the buried treasure you've been hoping for!" he said as he handed me the two necklaces covered in years of grime. After cleaning them and determining that they were real gold, I showed them to Joe. "These gold necklaces must have belonged to the Gunnings," I said. "Let's drive out to Yellow Springs and see if Nora would like to come to Young's Dairy Farm with us. We'll surprise her!" I said.

Young's Dairy Farm is an iconic landmark located just outside of the small bohemian village of Yellow Springs, home of the ultraliberal Antioch College. A working dairy farm since the late 1800s, the family-owned business started offering ice cream in the 1960s at their farm fresh store and an Ohio tradition was born. Over the years, they added a petting zoo, hayrides, and miniature golf, creating a destination that is especially great for people-watching in warm weather.

We picked up Nora in town and headed out for ice cream. "I've found a surprise for you," I told her, handing her the gold necklaces. She held the necklaces, closely examining them, and you could almost see her mind searching the long-lost files of her past. "My parents went to Greece and bought these necklaces for me and Grace. I had been playing with them in the Monk's Cell when they accidentally slipped behind a wall. No one was able to help me retrieve them," she said. So my quest for buried treasure was a success and brought back a piece of history and a fond memory to our friend Nora.

While awaiting the plumber's arrival, the covered walkway was rebuilt and the studio was resurrected. Joe designed a new walkway that integrated with the eastern end of the house at one end and attached to the studio to form an extended soffit on the other. Instead of several small rooms inside the studio, the space became one room with relocated windows along the zen garden, providing a view of the ravine beyond. "This can be your man cave!" I joked with Joe. "As long as you agree to keep your tools out of the house. Maybe this way, you'll organize them so you can find them when you need them." There were bins of tools for Joe to sort out, and I was hoping that in having a designated spot, one with a view no less, it would encourage him to organize his tools and prefer working out there instead of taking over the limited space in drawers and cabinets inside the house.

Knowing we were ready to finish the exterior of the studio and that we didn't have any skills in applying stucco, I made a suggestion. "I have an idea for the exterior of the new studio. What if we use board-and-batten cypress with a row of clerestory windows along the top to mimic the original carport that was attached to the house?" I asked. "We don't have the cypress and we would have to order clerestory windows," Joe replied back. "We have a supplier of cypress wood—that schoolteacher on the way to Oxford—and I saved the inoperable clerestory windows that had been in the kitchen. I hid them in the tower," I informed him. The original facade of the carport was a series of stucco piers that was not designed by the original trio. Since we had neither the skills nor a tradesman to stucco the exterior, it wasn't a hard sell. Adam's skills would come into play, fabricating the batten strips as well as the shiplap joint on the top of each board and the tongue and groove detail on the bottom to match the detail found on the house. The vertical windows that bordered the zen garden would have replacement pieces on the parts that were badly damaged by water and then returned to that façade, as would the repaired clerestory windows. A glass front door found leaning in the carport was installed for the studio entrance facing the road.

Having worked hard all summer, we decided to take a small break on an extended weekend to Detroit. Both kids are photographers, so I booked an urban exploration tour in August of 2015, which took participants through various abandoned buildings including factories, churches, schools, and libraries. Detroit was a mecca for abandoned architecture, so the tour was perfect for teenage photographers, as well as a welcomed reprieve from the heat and humidity. The decaying structures, adorned with beautiful graffiti art, were the perfect background for those with an interest in photography.

We also spent a day at Cranbrook Academy of Art, enjoying the architecture, which includes a nearby Frank Lloyd Wright home as well as two museums. Outside the Steven Holl-designed science museum was an outdoor garden that features a gabion wall behind a shallow water feature. Joe and I had admired the use of gabion walls, which are cages filled with rocks that are usually used for erosion controlling places where it is difficult for concrete to be poured. Recently, they have gotten an aesthetic cache, especially since their use at the Dominus Winery in the Napa Valley of California by the Swiss architects, Herzog and de Meuron.

"What if we use the leftover mountains of bluestone aggregate from beneath the old concrete floor and create a gabion wall outside the kitchen?" I suggested, referring to the four large mountains of stone that had been removed from the house and were piled high on the upper lawn. "We have to have the stone hauled away, so why not incorporate some of it into the design?"

Joe liked the idea, and when we returned home, he ordered cages to hold the rock. Since our stone was smaller in size than the usual gabion cages are designed to hold, he and Adam jury-rigged the cages with a shifted overlap of two grids to better contain our smaller rocks. They set up the cages, seven in total, with each cage being one foot deep, three feet long and three feet tall. I soon learned to hide the larger ugly rubble in the back section that lay adjacent to the concrete block wall, but the aggregate, approximately one inch by three inches, needed to be placed individually to lock them in a tight wedge. I would climb the stone hills piled in front of the house on the upper lawn, placing the best pieces into buckets, then carry them down the temporary ramp and proceed to carefully layer them into the cages. Adam computed that each of the seven cages would hold approximately 1,100 pounds of stone. That fall, my gabion wall came to completion and provided me with the most defined arm muscles of my life. Even the masons were impressed by the end results!

By late September of 2015, the plumbers had returned and proceeded to dig deep trenches into the ground within the house. Big Mike, Curt, and Danny became regular fixtures at the job site. Besides sports, the topics often revolved around hunting. I'd catch them eyeing the bucks that traveled regularly along the creek and told them "Don't even think about it!" I learned to judge a buck by the points on its antlers. That winter, one of the local bucks left me a gift, a nice set of four-point antlers near the pond.

Digging the trenches involved getting a small backhoe into the house. Adam created two openings, one through the outdoor cabinets in the kitchen patio into the dining room and the other through the framework around the casement windows into the 1940 breezeway between the living room and the future main bedroom. Big Mike effortlessly operated the machine into the small openings of the house, digging deep trenches without any structural incidents. When I told Big Mike that it had been a dream of mine to work a backhoe, he set it up on the upper lawn near the hills of rubble that had been extracted from beneath the floor, gave me a short lesson, and told me, "Go to town!" Operating the backhoe was not intuitive and much harder than I had anticipated. While Big Mike operated the machine with ease, I had the hardest time even moving rocks around the piles. My respect for the abilities of the trades grew with each job!

Our decision to use copper pipes for water supply was well worth the expense after discovering that PEX water supply lines potentially leeched carcinogens. The plumbing and heating expense was by far the largest expenditure—more than the temporary house we purchased and all the renovations we made to it! We tapped the city water line to provide water to both the house and tower. New sanitary waste lines were connected to the existing septic system.

A hydronic heating system is like a carefully made, multi-layer submarine sandwich, although one with an insane price tag. After the plumbing pipes came gravel backfill, then a passive radon system using perforated PVC pipe, a plastic vapor barrier, polyisocyanurate insulation board, an insulation blanket, and woven wire mesh to which a serpentine arrangement of small PEX tubing for glycol is attached with plastic snap ties. Finally, after all those layers, the concrete flooring can be poured.

Curt and Danny were then confined to the small basement to connect all the PEX tubing to pumps, to the boiler and to an elaborate control system for the seven different zones of the house. The basement stair is very steep, and my fear of ladders kept me upstairs, so Joe took a photograph of their work—an image so disturbing in its complexity that it entered my dream realm, haunting me like those nightmares of having to remember a forgotten locker combination!

On the winter solstice, the concrete truck and pumper arrived, digging up the partially frozen yard, leaving deep ruts several inches deep from the pumper that was parked on the front lawn. Joe and Adam oversaw the operation and along with the experienced team, manhandled the thick hose used to transport the concrete from the truck and pumper parked on the upper lawn. "You have no idea how difficult it is to direct the flow of the concrete. That big hose was like wrestling an anaconda, even with several guys!" Joe commented. The application was handled area by area, based on the elevation changes and logical separations starting at each end of the house. The showers have sloped floors so water would travel to the drains and thus were a separate pour, as was wherever there was an elevation change, which first required that Joe and Adam build several wood forms. The process took three separate workdays, ending just before the new year. I stayed away while the men worked, letting the photos Joe took suffice until the job was completed and temperatures increased.

After the concrete floor was poured, with its two-by-four gridded imprint that followed the original, then came the wall framing that would separate the rooms, the beginnings of the kitchen peninsula, and then the cabinetry for each of the bathrooms.

CHAPTER 11:
Future Layout

While waiting for the concrete floors to cure and the temperatures outside to rise, Joe finalized the layout of the rooms. With only one photograph of the original kitchen and a 1940 floor plan, we wanted to remain respectful of the original design but also reorganize features to meet our modern needs. The original shelving that ran along the stone wall in the kitchen would be rebuilt with a peninsula underneath, extending from where the Gunning's built-in dining table had been positioned. Instead of the original butcher block counters, long since removed and replaced with a faux marble plastic laminate by the second owners, a counter-height slab of soapstone with lower cabinets and seating for four would be in its place.

The countertop under the counter-level windows, the coffee station, and the dining room servery would also be topped with soapstone, with cabinets finished in cypress to mimic those seen in the original kitchen photograph. Beneath the strip of counter-level glass would be a trough for small houseplants. The appliances and backsplash would be stainless steel. Around the raised kitchen ceiling, the original cypress soffit band would be restored. Where the 1940s "workspace" had been a galley kitchen, we repositioned the refrigerator from its previous arrangement, opening a new passage near the kitchen patio door into the dining room. The reconfiguration allowed direct access to the dining room while affording additional light to enter the dark, north-facing kitchen.

The large open space extending beyond the kitchen, termed the "lounge" on the original floor plan, would become our dining room. We enjoy entertaining and the wall of French doors would offer dinner guests a wonderful view of the ravine. The angled fireplace that oriented to both the kitchen and the dining room would provide warmth as well as a wonderful visual aesthetic. We moved the west wall of the dining room by four feet on the two-by-four-foot grid, borrowing from the adjacent bedroom so that we could place a table that would seat eight. The larger room would offer wooded views from the four pairs of French doors, as well as a new north-facing window for the dining room, while still maintaining one of the pairs of the French doors for the bedroom.

Terminating the line of ravine-facing French doors was the mitered glass corner window in the western bedroom. For privacy without obstructing the view, a four-foot pocket door was to be installed. The bedroom would feature an open bathroom with the toilet and shower tucked around a corner for privacy. The coarse-cut stone shower would double in size due to the elimination of a former separate water heater for this 1960 addition. A recess in the shower's stone wall, where a wall dividing the shower from the small water heater closet once stood, would be filled and grouted with small stones collected from the creek. The sink vanity of restored cypress butcher block, original to the room, would have a new stainless sink to replace the one that was stolen. Beyond the vanity was a waist-level corner window with a restored frame and new insulating glass for energy efficiency. Outside the window was a collection of arranged river stone above a catch basin that dissipated water from the roof-edge gutter with the lofty spruce trees in the background.

A short hallway along the glass exterior stepped down two steps from the dining room to the Point Room, pointing southward and extending out to the ravine like the prow of a ship. A bank of tall French doors lined one side, positioned just above an exterior planter faced in stone that cantilevered off the house. The interior enclosure for the room was formed by the stone of the house's central core of three fireplaces. Unfortunately, the fireplace in the Point Room never functioned properly due to the proportions of the hearth and firebox. Inside this room were two steps back up to a platform for the bed and the level of the adjoining bathroom. Joe modestly extended the platform to allow the proper length for a bed to be positioned with a commanding view down the creek. The skylight positioned over the head of the bed would allow stargazing before falling asleep. In the winter months, with no foliage on the trees, one could watch the sun travel across the horizon from sunrise to sunset.

The stone wall continued through a doorway that formed the walls of a bathroom that was illuminated by operable clerestory windows and divided into three zones: a washbasin area, a toilet alcove, and an area with the original small peach-colored tub completely enveloped by ten-foot-high stone walls. Since the original sink and faucets had been stolen, we purchased a granite boulder vessel sink for the top of the vanity that Joe would design. A restored closet and built-in drawers on one wall led to a doorway connecting back to the kitchen, near the front entrance. As the only bathroom not within a bedroom with actual doors for privacy, this bathroom would serve the Point Room and our guests.

The large room to the left as you entered the main entrance was termed the "dormitory" on original plans; it was meant as a bedroom for the Gunning children. The remnants of a doorframe indicated that there was once a Dutch door at the narrow opening into this room. This would allow Mrs. Gunning to close the lower half of the door while keeping an eye and ear on the children while they played. We decided to keep this doorframe as a relic. This room had been used as a living room for several decades and would serve the same function in the future.

The ceilings of the sixteen-by-twenty-four-foot room were a low seven feet, and they lacked the dramatic effect from the change in height one experienced when entering the kitchen. Three bays of floor-to-ceiling, stacked horizontal windows, divided by rusticated stone piers that extended beyond the windows to support the cantilevered roof outside, were intended to frame three children's beds for the number of children the Gunnings intended to have. The easternmost bay contained a built-in sofa made in the late 1940s of plywood and cypress board, which was removed during construction for restoration. The top frame of the sofa was scribed to fit the irregularities of the stone pier, then extended four feet beyond with an attached side table on the end. A third stone fireplace, angled to match the geometry of the adjacent Point Room, was the focal point of the room. Tucked into a nook behind the fireplace was a cypress desk with floating shelves above. The height of the desk was only twenty-five inches, too low for adult use, so Joe would eventually incorporate the original design into a functional computer station workspace. Along the front of the house were built-in closets, just below the horizontal wall of clerestory windows. With our need for a place for the television and stereo, Joe decided to remove the closets, leaving the wall for artwork and for low cabinets he would later design and fabricate.

Behind the built-in sofa was a step down to a small triangular space that was once a breezeway between the dormitory and the original 1940 carport. A double casement window along the front, and a pair of French doors with a fixed pane of glass adjacent to it along the ravine side, provided light and ventilation. The original pair of French doors were relocated to the dining room in order to have a continuous and consistent line of doors from the same period along the ravine side, which was their original configuration in the smaller 1940 footprint.

The original carport had been transformed into two small children's bedrooms with a small bathroom and a laundry area in the late 1940s. When we took ownership, the walls that divided the space had been removed, leaving an irregular strip of old caulking on the stone wall where the separation once occurred. This large room, to which several support posts had been added to prevent the roof from collapsing, would become our bedroom suite, with its peaceful views of both the wooded ravine and the eventual zen garden. Along the front of the house, on an elevated concrete platform that once provided storage in the carport, Joe would design a wall of built-in cabinets that would house one of the air conditioning units, as well as our closet and drawers, leaving the platform bed as the only furniture in the bedroom. Opposite the wall of cabinets would be a utility sink, washer, and dryer. Along the wall that separated this space from the bedroom suite would be the low bed that Joe had designed forty years earlier. It would have a view through the new seven-foot casement windows that replaced the old, inoperable, fixed plate glass.

Beyond the bed would be a raised plinth, housing an air-jet tub and sink cabinetry suspended from the ceiling in a compatible design theme that was carried throughout the house. The surface of the sink and tub enclosure would feature the large ceramic tiles utilized in the other bathrooms in the house. These tiles matched the midrange warm gray of the stone and would be used for the shower and toilet enclosure. Below the ceiling-mounted medicine cabinets with mirrored fronts would be two granite boulder vessel sinks, resting on the plinth they shared with the tub.

Although we had already purchased the granite boulder wash basins, which Joe dubbed "Flintstone Moderne," late in 2015, we began ordering fixtures that the plumbers would soon install. In going over his invoices, I came across one that seemed to contain a mistake. "Joe, this plumbing fixture invoice has an obvious error on it. It shows a toilet triple the cost of the other two, and the other two were costly Duravit fixtures!" I pointed out. "Oh yeah, I meant to tell you about that. I found this beautiful rectilinear one-piece toilet that works really well with the design theme," he started to explain. "Joe, it's a frickin' toilet, in our bathroom, that no one will ever see but us!" I turned to Adam, hoping for some moral support on this outrageous expense. "Adam, did you see how expensive this toilet was that Joe ordered?" Adam laughed and threw his arms up. "I'm staying out of this one!" he said, shaking his head. "I guess the king of the house needs his throne!" he chuckled. From that point on, that toilet became known as Joe's "throne."

The extravagances didn't end with the toilet. Joe's "throne" entitled me to a lifetime of leverage on whatever expensive piece I couldn't live without. My first request was for the fabrication of a narrow slit window, three and a half inches wide by eighty inches tall, that extended beyond the stone wall in our bedroom suite. As a cost reduction, Joe had pulled the exterior wall inward so it aligned with the adjacent stone wall, which eliminated the little jog at the juncture that created the tiny window. "No one will ever know it's gone," he commented. "You got your throne, I want my slit window!" I insisted, and I won. Adam fabricated a frame that he scribed to engage the irregularities of the stone wall. When the narrow piece of insulating glass arrived and it was time to install it, they allowed me the honor of installing it in its place!

During that period, Joe inventoried the Douglas fir plywood panels deemed salvable in order to calculate how much plywood we would need to order to replace the damaged pieces. We wanted to match the original Douglas fir but could not find plywood that had the scale, character, and figure of the grain that mid-century plywood had. My main request was that I did not want knots visible in the plywood, "I can't live with polka-dotted walls and ceilings!" I commented. This meant that we needed a better grade of plywood, the kind usually found in hardwood veneers, not in fir or pine. Our solution was to use birch veneer plywood, which was not a big hit to the budget and has a grain that is very close in appearance to the old Douglas fir common in 1940.

From the salvaged two-by-four-foot ceiling panels, Joe designed a pattern that utilized the dark salvaged panels above the beds in each bedroom. He was also able to recycle much of the weathered cypress fascia boards as accent walls in each bedroom. These boards were originally the fascias of the overhangs along the edges of the roof. Years of water damage had rotted away much of their backsides, which rendered them unsuitable for reuse, so we were able to piece together the usable sections to create beautiful, weathered-wood interior finishes, saving them from ending up in a landfill.

Since these cypress fascia boards were already distressed, it made sense to also utilize them for the base of the kitchen peninsula where shoes would scuff them. Most of the original Douglas fir plywood wall panels were badly delaminated from their wicking of water in the numerous floor flooding events of the past. Many of them had suffered a similar fate at the top from roof leaks. The only original wall panels that were salvageable were in the central area of the house that included the kitchen wall across from the entrance, the central bathroom, and behind the desk in the dormitory/living room. All the other walls would be reclad in birch veneer plywood (raised one-half inch off the floors as an added precaution) with a concealed detail that Adam routed into their tops to allow us to suspend artwork on wires from little "S" hooks Joe found online at an art gallery supply company. The grade A birch finish was much lighter than the seventy-five-year-old finish on the salvaged Douglas fir, which we suspected had darkened both the varnish and the wood itself from exposure to ultraviolet light over the decades. Justification came from the only vintage color photograph—one of the kitchen that indicated a lighter original finish that was varnished, unstained plywood that had grown darker from the passage of time.

The house had never had air-conditioning, and I felt it stayed sufficiently cool in the summer, as it was shaded by the canopy of mature trees, with cooling breezes rising from the moving water of the creek and a strategy of ventilating the house at night and closing it up in the morning. Joe, however, did not want to risk the opportunity to conceal AC units, knowing of the ugly and awkwardly placed mini split systems we had seen added later in other houses. "We hopefully don't have to use it, but now is the time to conceal the units so we don't have to see those clunky white boxes on our beautiful wood walls. I also worry about dampness and humidity creating problems without AC." The downside was losing closet space in both the Point Room and main bedroom closet, with one also placed in a storage closet on the kitchen patio. Of course, the expense was also an issue in a budget that was rapidly spiraling out of control.

We knew restoration was expensive, but we had always assumed that if need be, we could tap into the equity on both the house we were temporarily living in during construction, as well as Glenbrow. Having recently sold the Noverre Musson house, restored over a fifteen-year period, we started the new project with no debt. We paid cash for the small house we purchased in order to remain in our daughters' school district during restoration, as well as for Glenbrow. After closing on both properties, we also sold the lot we intended to build a new house on prior to finding Glenbrow to the developer who had knocked auspiciously on the door. We were mistaken in assuming the ease in borrowing on our equity in both properties. After the 2008 financial crisis, borrowing became difficult, even with good credit. Although we were able to get a line of credit using the temporary house, the appraised value was less than half of what we sold it for a year later. Banks were being cautious, and we could find no one in Columbus who was interested in allowing us to borrow against the equity we had invested in Glenbrow. We were quickly running out of funds. Restoring a ruin is very expensive, even when you have done it several times before and do a lot of the work yourself. It is definitely not for the faint of heart. Luckily, we had Joe's salary, had learned to live frugally, and we knew we would eventually receive funds once we were able to move out of the temporary house.

CHAPTER 12:
Recreating a
Modern Garden

S pring of 2016 arrived in all its verdant glory with a colorful array of blossoms. The tips of the daffodils first emerge in late February, even though we can still expect more snow. The sound of the songbirds marks the awakening, chirping as they toss the decaying leaves on the ravine hillside with their beaks in search of worms while the ground is still frozen. Tips of chartreuse sprout from the branches of honeysuckle bushes while the trees begin to bud overhead. Hibernating animals emerge from their dens, searching for food after their long winter sleep. Great blue herons return from the south, stretching their broad wingspans as they glide gracefully above the snaking creek. First to bloom are the snowdrops and crocuses. Later, daffodils, forsythia, lilac, magnolia, rhododendrons, azalea—all mixed in with the various native wildflowers—wash away the dull gloom of winter. Despite the upheaval of construction, the beauty of spring reminded us of why we purchased the dilapidated property in the first place.

All the landscape work Maren and I had accomplished the previous year, cutting down vines and invasive shrubs, provided us with a splendid view of the ravine's rebirth after the long cold winter. Clearing away brush allowed us to witness the striated layers of vegetation on the slope of the ravine. At the bottom, near the creek's edge, were the Virginia bluebells—bright blue in a field of green. Nearby, bright yellow trout lilies bowed downward between their mottled leaves. Next were the tall, palmate-leafed mayapples, with a singular flower peeking out from underneath their leaves. Further uphill were the tiny periwinkle blossoms of the vinca vines. Scattered throughout were redbuds, lilac, barrenwort, and trillium. Soon the entire ravine had sprung back to life!

During the fall and winter, we also cleared the tennis court of fallen branches and ivy that had covered the forlorn hardscape. This allowed for the sedum growing there to flourish. The chartreuse colored succulent blossomed in vivid yellow. We had cut the surrounding grassy edges of the court the previous year but decided to allow the prairie to flourish, with just a pathway for watering plants and a trail through the spruce grove connected to the road. The tennis court, reclaimed by nature as trees were growing through cracks in the pavement, would eventually become an excellent place for our outdoor furniture.

The ground beyond the court was low and tended to be swampy, making it the perfect site for the deciduous bald cypress tree, its knobby knees planted firmly in the ground as it extended some fifty feet up to the sky. A tall skeleton in the winter, it budded in mid-April when its light green feathery foliage reappeared. Near its base, the long pink canes of raspberry bramble arched forward with sharp barbs protecting the stems. Invasive English ivy, Virginia creeper, and honeysuckle peeked out from underneath layers of feathery orange foliage from last season—all of them would be future eradication projects.

About fifteen feet away from the court's edge was a fence separating Glenbrow from recent suburban development. Joe and the kids had planted a metasequoia near the mature cypress the previous year for Mother's Day. Chosen in part for its preference for wet soil, the deciduous tree is also known for its fast growth. Metasequoias, also known as dawn redwoods, can grow over five feet per year, so the houses could be blocked from view within a few short years. Closely related to cypress trees, the tree was also selected due to their history. Metasequoias were once common in the northern hemisphere, but they were thought to be extinct until 1941, when a grove was rediscovered in a remote area of China. 1941 was the year that the Gunnings moved into Glenbrow.

The decision to allow the area surrounding the tennis court to revert to prairie was a wise one. Soon, besides the tall prairie grasses, the area filled with Queen Anne's Lace, daisies, asters, and goldenrod, creating a habitat for the birds and bees to enjoy. It also created a picturesque backdrop for future outdoor dining.

Almost the entire upper lawn near the house had hills of dirt, stone, and aggregate excavated from beneath the concrete floor, piled up to about six feet tall and extending across what had once been a grassy area. To get to the tennis court from the house, you had to climb the rugged surface of the hills before descending back down the other side. Since the excavation below the concrete floor was complete and my gabion wall baskets filled, it was time to have these mounds of remaining rubble hauled away. We hired the concrete contractor to remove the piles.

In between hauling away the truckloads, I had access to the front-end loader and its driver, so I decided to have him relocate some boulders from the far end of the tennis court that had been covered in vines. I had them moved to form a circle in a clearing just beyond the western bedroom to form a fire pit. The day was chilly, and upon seeing my plan come to fruition, Adam said, "Let's put that sucker to use!" He piled small pieces of scrap wood from framing work into the pit and almost immediately had a fire going. "Did I ever tell you about my buddy, Tim?" Of course he had, but I enjoyed his descriptive tales of work sites past with their cast of characters. "That guy was a firebug and they ended up burning down the construction site," Adam continued, as the flames sprang to life. "Well, that's why our pit is away from the house and near the well!" I replied back.

With the mountains of rubble removed, a large stretch of dirt, rutted from both the arborists and the heavy concrete trucks, ran almost the entire length of the house. We had topsoil brought in, and the kids and I spread the dirt, then seeded it so that we could grow grass before the hot weather set in, using the well for water. The sky was clear, and the temperature was warm, so when I returned from an errand, I found the kids battling each other with the hose and buckets of water. At least the seed was getting watered!

I didn't care whether or not we ever had a perfect lawn, but anything was better than the current mud in wet weather and dust when it was dry. As much as I loved the prairie and its wildflowers, we needed a mowed area for the dogs. The grass came in, along with dandelions and other native plants, but the vegetation that seemed to do the best was clover. I didn't mind, since the bees liked it and it was effective in preventing erosion. I used a dandelion tool to pull thistle out but allowed whatever else that would grow to flourish.

After previously discovering that Glenbrow was listed with the Cultural Landscape Foundation under the category "Modern Garden" and "Estate," I felt a sense of responsibility to bring the landscape back to its former glory, embracing its rustic beauty over a pristine garden. This responsibility came with a lot of maintenance work. It was easy to lose track of time while weeding, distracted by new discoveries as simple as a new mushroom I had never encountered before or finding a skink upon lifting a rock. There were more microenvironments to explore on our two-and-a-half-acre property than I could ever imagine. From the creek-side bedrock environment, to the flourishing growth around the pond, to the decomposing ash trees along the ravine, the property was a wealth of life-forms to explore.

While the men were working inside, I took advantage of having the kids available to tackle finishing the zen garden—the area surrounded on three sides by the studio/carport, walkway, and our bedroom suite. With large, stacked boulders as its main focus, and the established hostas I uncovered along one side of the curved stone retaining wall, I devised a design that featured both dark gray, smooth Mexican river stone and cream-colored pebbles. Originally, I thought about creating a true zen garden that one could rake, but after learning poultry grit was used in traditional gardens and knowing there were feral cats nearby, I selected cream-colored pebbles so it would not become a giant litter box. Before the stone could be added, we needed to pull the weeds, then lay weed fabric down to prevent them from reappearing between the stones. There were a lot of weeds to pull before the fabric could be laid and attached to the ground with metal landscape pins.

When the temperatures rose, Maren and her friend Alex switched from the carport work to rebuild the collapsed retaining wall between the ravine and the stone patio outside of our future bedroom. This area was in perpetual shade while the summer foliage was overhead. A segment of the wall had been removed to allow Adam and the plumbers access to the ravine side of the house, and we wanted to protect the unearthed stone patio from erosion. The wall, perhaps four and a half feet tall, was stacked in layers of stone that leaned back to better retain the higher ground of the stone patio.

The shade of the trees and the water flowing in the creek created a gentle cool breeze on hot days. After one heavy summer rain, the fast-moving water created rapids so strong that several large boulders approximately three feet in diameter appeared from upstream, deposited in view of our dining room. When the water subsided, we placed heavy, wedge-shaped stones behind the boulders to prevent them from traveling further downstream in the future.

To cool off during breaks, the kids would occasionally remove their work boots and socks to wade downstream to explore. The suburban development to our west had been built in the mid 1990s, with the homes further downstream lining the edge of the ravine. One day, after the rampant creek had subsided, the kids reported that one of the backyards had collapsed and been washed away, leaving an eroded cliff exposing the foundation of the house. It reminded us that we needed to be mindful of the force of rainwater in a heavy rain, especially with our dogs.

There was abundant wildlife on the property. The continual noise of power saws and nail guns kept most animals at bay during the workday, but in the mornings, deer scat and other droppings reminded us that they were nearby. The pond was full of goldfish, bullfrogs, turtles, and northern water snakes. The snakes and turtles would comingle on a partially submerged boulder on the far side on the pond, warming themselves in the afternoon sun. Blue jays and dragonflies skirted the water's surface, occasionally dropping to feed. In the evening, the bullfrogs chorused the surroundings, calling out for mates. On occasion, the snakes would slip slowly from the rocks into the calm water to swim along the surface edge in search of food. Upon approach, the bullfrogs would jump into deeper water, eluding the snakes. Overhead, hawks would soar, gliding high above the treetops, until murders of crows chased them away.

Stacked canal stones, mottled brown in color, each approximately four feet long, bordered a section of the pond, creating a raised surface. Dozens of yucca plants grew along the edges and out along the rocky banks of the pond. In late May, a long single stem arose from each plant, producing white flowers that looked like a giant lily of the valley. In the early morning, black snakes, several feet long, could be found underneath the yuccas, coiled with thick bulges in their midsections and convulsing with peristaltic waves as they digested their prey from the night before. The snakes were never aggressive and kept the rodent population under control. Although an unexpected encounter with one of the snakes might be startling, I appreciated that they were part of our ecosystem. Likewise, the bullfrogs, with their appetite for insects, left the surroundings virtually free of mosquitoes.

The harmonious peace was occasionally disturbed by violence. After returning from an errand one day, I discovered Adam, Maren, and Alex with sticks and shovels near the pond's edge. "What are you guys doing?" I asked. "Two snakes were fighting over a bullfrog and we're trying to save it!" They pushed one of the snakes away and I seemed to catch eyes with the bullfrog as it submerged for the final time within the grasp of the victor. It was a sad reminder that within the beauty of nature, there needs to be cruelty for survival.

Inside, the house was fitted with recessed LED light fixtures surrounded by a similar square wood frame as the originals, although they were remade in birch to match the new ceiling panels. New under-counter and soffit uplights in the kitchen were also LED fixtures for energy efficiency, as were the fixtures above the medicine cabinets in each of the bathrooms. The exception was over the peninsula, where we reused a set of Italian low-voltage cable lights that we had purchased years before as a ten-year anniversary present to each other, and a new pendant light from the same manufacturer, over the dining table. I had first seen these fixtures, which reminded me of a cross between a Calder mobile and a fishing bobber, in a Los Angeles gallery years before and immediately fell in love with them. For sentimental reasons, I removed them prior to placing our old Noverre Musson house on the market, with the intention of using them in the new home.

Once the plywood arrived, we set up assembly lines with Joe and Adam cutting the chamfered-edged pieces while the kids and I applied layers of polyurethane with a light sanding between the layers. I had assumed installing the panels would move quickly, but we soon realized that the standard two-by-four panels would need slight adjustments and each adjustment required us to cut new chamfered edges and apply more urethane.

At the end of the summer, we learned the sad news that the youngest of Rob and Mary Gunning's children, Seth, had passed away. A memorial service was held at a nearby forest preserve, and we invited the extended family and their friends to visit the house afterward. Grace's daughter, Johnnie Day Durand, played a hauntingly beautiful rendition of *Moon River* on a musical saw as people gathered. Instead of a mournful event, it was a celebration of fond memories of their brother and friend. Those who visited the house afterward shared recollections of days gone by as we toured the rooms. When we reached the Point Room bathroom, Tom, the jovial David Crosby look-alike, told the story of how his mother was pregnant with him when a black snake emerged from the drain while she was bathing, causing her to go into labor. "Yikes! We won't mention that one to Fia!" I joked.

After the kids returned to school, we had the stonemasons return and relay the stone base under the covered walkway along the planter. There was some upheaval of large pieces of cracked concrete that needed to be removed and replaced with stone blocks from the pile they had earlier found in the local stone yard. Joe also had them mortar the loose flagstones around the perimeter of our future bedroom; they had been removed for the addition of a trench drain. Their work looked great, but it had caused ruts and destroyed the weed fabric I had laid in the zen garden. It didn't take long before new weeds poked through the openings. "I shouldn't have started that project when I did. Now I'm going to have to pull up all the torn weed fabric, weed again, and lay new fabric. Ugh!" I told Joe. "At least I hadn't filled it with pebbles yet. That would have been a disaster!" In my frustration, I decided to focus on other tasks that I wouldn't have to repeat until I was sure that work around the area was completely finished.

Joe and Adam continued the tedious task of installing the ceiling panels. Frustrated with needing to redo my work in the zen garden, I offered to help them inside. Originally, we thought each panel would be a consistent two-by-four rectangle, but we soon realized slight alterations would be necessary to keep the overall grid in alignment. The raised section of the kitchen and the cramped Point Room bathroom were difficult due to height, but by far the most difficult pieces to install were the multisided panels in the eastern bedroom suite. One of the panels around the ceiling-suspended medicine cabinets had twenty-two sides, including the small notches at the supports, each of them needing additional cuts and refinishing with each edge revision.

Adam built a "T" shaped prop based on the ceiling height for me to hold the panels in place and covered it with an old Green Bay Packers sweatshirt to protect the panels. "Adam, being a Chicago Bears fan, I feel like a traitor hoisting this sweatshirt up in the air!" I told him. "Think of it as a destroyed shirt on its way to its final resting place," Joe reminded me.

After making the appropriate alterations needed for the panel to fit, each time adding a new chamfered edge to the minor correction, the covered "T" would hold the panel in place and Adam would declare, "shoot the shit out of it!"—his way of signaling to Joe that it was time for his vintage nail gun. Joe had never used a nail gun before, but after using Adam's, he went out and purchased his own. "I can't even imagine how many nails those guys drove by hand in building this house!" he said.

By Christmas of 2016, the house looked almost ready to move in, with the wall and ceiling panels installed, light fixtures mounted, and cabinets in place, although without their fronts or countertops. For countertops, I wanted to avoid the butcher block that was original to the house after witnessing how distressed it looked in the rarely used kitchen of our Noverre Musson house. Also, the cypress butcher block on the vanity of the western bedroom from 1964 was marked and stained—a look I wanted to avoid seeing in my kitchen, which would get heavy use. I researched other options from the period and thought period appropriate stainless-steel countertops would be clean and would reflect the light nicely, but Joe nixed the idea after specifying it in his architecture firm's kitchenette. "Our counters there were dinged and scratched within a few weeks," he complained. We both liked soapstone, but wanted to avoid any with a green cast, preferring black instead. We had searched several stone yards in Central Ohio for soapstone but discovered that they were passing off a polished dark color marble or granite look-alike in its place. Just after Christmas, the kids and I traveled to southern Indiana to a fabricator that specialized in soapstone and selected a black piece that reminded me of the gestural marks of hand sketching throughout its surface. The trip allowed me to pick out a piece that I absolutely loved. The stone was cut and installed in no time. Soon we began massaging food grade mineral oil into the cold hard surface, bringing out the rich features of the stone.

To save money, we purchased a vintage professional Viking range and hood from a former chef's house, getting a deal that was cheaper than buying a low-end range from a big box store. I had wanted a stainless professional range, and this allowed me to have one, practicing reuse while saving dwindling resources. Although I was nervous about getting the large stainless range down the steps and into the house without incident, our movers had no difficulty. They were able to maneuver it through the removable wall in the dining room without damage to any of the woodwork. After Joe and Adam hooked up the range, we discovered one issue—the matching Viking hood would not fit with the low seven-foot ceilings above the stove. We purchased a new stainless hood to fit in its place—another unexpected expense.

As we neared the finish line, we were quickly depleting our remaining resources. "We'll get through this!" Joe kept reminding me. "Once we sell the Bexley house, we'll be fine financially, and we will live in our dream house." The catch was that we couldn't sell our Bexley house until we received an occupancy permit, and we had to finish a few expensive things in the house before we could schedule our final inspection. The electrical work was not complete, smoke detectors were yet to be installed, and tile in bathrooms was unfinished—all are required for occupancy. In addition, there were no door fronts on any of our kitchen cabinets and we still needed to purchase a refrigerator.

After many sleepless nights, out of the blue, we found a savior. Joe had explained our situation to a financial planner who was trying to market his services. He recommended a former colleague who was working in a small town in rural Ohio. After Joe met with the banker, they sent out an appraiser to determine the value of Glenbrow. While we had initially been confident that there would not be difficulty in completing the project, our experience in post-Great Recession America left us nervously awaiting the appraisal. We were pleasantly surprised when the appraisal came back six times more than we needed, despite the unfinished condition of the house, enabling us to finish without the stress of sleepless nights. "See, I told you it would all work out!" Joe replied when he received the appraisal. The additional funds would allow us to finish the project and the loan would be repaid when we sold the house we were living in during the restoration.

The electrician returned to complete his work and installed the interconnected smoke and carbon monoxide detectors that can communicate with smartphones. Joe had originally framed for the dimensions of a subzero refrigerator, but it had been over fifteen years since we had purchased our last one, and sticker shock, coupled with the ballooning budget overruns, had me search for a comparable-sized, counter-depth refrigerator that would fit into the housing the guys had built but at a much lower cost. The restoration had taught us to live without frivolities.

CHAPTER 13:
The Move

S pring returned, and while I was eager to return to landscaping, the daunting task of preparing for the move was foisted upon my shoulders. Although I had made significant progress with downsizing during our initial move from the 5,400-square-foot Noverre Musson house, my family has some dominant hoarder genes that run through Joe's lineage! It was difficult to get Joe and the kids to part with their accumulated stuff. Joe is a collector—art, books, CDs, tools. You name it, he collected it. Although our children were young adults away at college and soon to be permanently leaving the nest, they likewise were unwilling to part with their toys, books, and other relics of childhood. "We are going Usonian," I would tell them. "It entails becoming less materialistic." I would repeatedly remind them that the small basement was only large enough for the hydronic system and nothing else and that our bedrooms had minimal closet space. I purchased platform beds with drawers underneath for clothing storage, but the small rooms still would not house what the large walk-out basement and extended closets once did.

Shelving was added to the studio in the carport for storage bins, but the idea was for that space to be used as Joe's workshop. I made numerous trips to Goodwill and Habitat for Humanity to further downsize. Every trip to the property was made with a carload of storage bins and piles of books, as we moved closer to moving into our new home. Several rows of bookshelves were added along the full length of the western bedroom to help accommodate our collection of architecture and art books, while Joe took many others to the ample bookshelves at his office. "Eventually, the tower lower level will have a wall of built-in bookshelves," Joe would remind me when I encouraged him to donate some of them.

With the loan now in place to cover our expenses until the temporary house was sold, we decided to move into Glenbrow before listing our house. Bexley was a community with excellent schools, and the price point we were planning to list the house at would be attractive for entry-level homeowners, so I wanted to make sure we had our certificate of occupancy before placing our house on the market. As luck would have it, we soon encountered an obstacle. Initially, the house was in an unincorporated section of Jefferson Township, but they were not able to provide a tap to the water main in front of our property, so we had annexed into the City of Reynoldsburg to have access to city water. Our building permit had been through Franklin County, as was standard for unincorporated properties, but now in Reynoldsburg, the requirement was to use their city permits. They didn't want to honor the Franklin County permits, while Franklin County, no longer having jurisdiction, could no longer issue our certificate of occupancy. Bureaucracy! Eventually it was resolved, we received the permit and immediately scheduled the movers.

In our cost-minding mode, we purchased Ikea beds for the kids' rooms, which, of course, needed to be assembled. Maren and I tackled the two beds during her spring break, setting up the minimalist birch platform beds with drawers below the mattresses in both the Point Room and the western bedroom so we wouldn't need to wait for moving trucks. There was definitely some swearing along the way, as is always case in assembling Ikea furniture! As frustrating as their instructions can be, we were thankful the two beds were identical—we benefited from our learning curve on the second one! Maren was returning to school for her final semester and would be living at Glenbrow when she moved back from school after graduation. During her entire four-year span of college, we had bought, restored, and now would be living at the site.

The house was devoid of most of our furniture. Our bedroom suite was empty, bins were stacked high, awaiting to be emptied, and there were no doors on any of the cabinets, but we were so excited to move in it didn't matter. After dinner at the Bexley house, cluttered with boxes awaiting the movers, we packed a bag with our toiletries, corralled the dogs and their respective beds, and after four years of hard work, we headed out to spend our first night at Glenbrow! We brought a special bottle of wine to christen our new home!

We arrived at Glenbrow at early twilight since the walkway lights were not yet installed, with both cars loaded to the brim with dogs and packed supplies. The property was so peaceful after three years of hearing the constant pounding of hammers and the buzzing of saws. It was the end of March 2017, the air was chilly outside, but inside, the warmth of the hydronic heat made the house cozy and inviting.

As we were still awaiting the movers, the furnishings were sparse, with only stools along the kitchen island and eight Eames chairs without a table in the dining room. Artwork, wrapped in heavy plastic, leaned against the walls, and our kitchen cabinets had minimal utensils and no doors. I had moved our Fiestaware to the kitchen shelves along the stone wall so that the pop of bright color reminded us the house was no longer a construction site! Earlier in the day, I made the bed in the western bedroom, so along with the books on the shelves, at least that room looked inviting.

The dogs were curious and excited, moving from room to room to explore their new home. The warmth of the concrete floors was surely soothing to Whisper's old bones and she seemed happy to be removed from the slippery bamboo floors of the temporary house. "Finally, what we've been waiting for, for so many years!" I exclaimed. "I'm so glad that Whisper lived long enough to move in." Whisper was a fifteen-and-a-half-year-old border collie-mix whose eyes and ears were failing, but she still had the stamina to go on short walks and greet us every day. Her heightened sense of smell would revel in all the new scents that a wooded setting offered. Lola Bola was bouncing from room to room, enjoying her perch overlooking the ravine. With foliage still absent, she had a full vista of both the creek and the woods from several rooms. Soon, there were nose-level markings on every window along the ravine. "She'll get used to it," I reminded Joe, as her loud barking echoed in the empty rooms.

To celebrate, we opened a bottle of Vernaccia di San Gimignano from a Tuscan hill town known for its numerous towers that we had visited on our honeymoon. Now we were settling atop our own hillside with our own tower, although that project would be a somewhat distant phase two. Tonight, we were thankful of the beautiful house that we now called home.

As the sun set, darkness filled the landscape, interrupted only by the distant lights from the houses across the ravine. Foliage would soon block any visual contact with our neighbors, but for now it was a reminder that we were in the proximity of suburbia. "We will definitely need to get drapes for our bedroom, especially since our bathroom is open!" I reminded Joe. "Although we won't need them once the leaves return."

We hooked up the dogs for "last call" before bedtime. Both dogs were excited by all the exotic new smells, with Lola pulling me toward the ravine. The sky was clear and dark, with no moonbeams to illuminate the grounds. Above us, stars filled the sky. There was some traffic noise apparent, as was the barking of distant dogs that were making their presence known from across the ravine, but it was still too early to hear the chorus of bullfrogs that we knew would soon greet us each evening. Although the dogs would have been happy to linger in the chilly air, our bodies were tired from moving books, so we decided it was time for bed. Lola Bola had other plans. She was too excited for bed, running from room to room, using her night vision to protect her new home from any possible threats that might be infiltrating the premises. "It's her first night. She'll settle down!" I kept reminding Joe.

At dawn, I arose to the familiar screeches of the red-tailed hawk nesting in the crown of the white branches of a tall sycamore tree on the other side of the ravine. Squawking crows, forever in an epic battle with the hawks, followed. I picked up the binoculars that I had laid on the floor and marveled at the view I enjoyed from the comfort of bed.

We drank our morning coffee while walking the dogs around the property. Elderly Whisper seemed to have a little pep in her step and Lola Bola was riled beyond belief, focused on a groundhog that lived near the septic system. It was chilly, but early hints of green were emerging, breaking through the carpet of dried leaves and tips of the honeysuckle. The songbirds let their presence be known as they erased the noisy traffic sound of the commuters just beyond our borders. Soon reality hit, reminding us that Joe needed to be one of them! He soon left for work while I began the daunting task of packing our previous residence for the move and preparing that house for sale.

Besides packing, I also needed to move some bushes, trees, and plants that were sentimental. Before selling our empty lot, I had transferred a magnolia, rhododendrons, azaleas and large-leaf hostas I'd received over the years as Mother's Day presents to the south Bexley yard. Now I needed to transfer them once again, before we placed the house on the market, so that their beauty would enhance Glenbrow.

To make way for the relocated bushes, I decided to clear some brush and tangles of invasive honeysuckle away from the edges of the mature Norway spruce trees. Their long horizontal branches reached over twenty-five feet in length, bending low to rest on the ground before arching back toward the sky. In the cleared-out spaces between the boughs, I replanted several of my bushes. Adding a mixture of rhododendrons and azaleas in the dappled sunlight between these branches would add a pop of bright pink in the spring, while their long coriaceous leaves would remain green and add visual texture in the winter. Across from the spruces, toward the road, was the copse of deciduous trees that screened the view of traffic racing along the road. Oak, cherry, and cottonwood trees made up the majority of the growth, with pines and mature yews along the frontage and burning bushes and blackberry bramble populating the outskirts. With sun in both morning and late afternoon, I thought this would be a perfect place for my magnolia tree, whose white spring flowers would bloom above clusters of daffodils that had been planted in the distant past. In between the spruce and deciduous trees was a pathway to the former tennis court and the twenty-foot-tall trees growing through the many cracks in its surface. We decided to set up our teak dining table and umbrella underneath a tree on the hard court.

On days when the spring rains made my trips difficult, I spent the day unpacking the numerous bins that I had stacked high along the walls. I hadn't spent much time alone inside the house prior to the move unless I was working, because I didn't want to get in the way of the workers and the various levels of construction mess surrounding them. Without the shrill sounds of saws, the intensely loud compressor motor accompanied by the pops of pneumatic nail guns, and the ubiquitous sports radio, the silence was a welcome relief. With the kids still away at college and Joe at work, I had the house to myself—just me and the pups, free to explore our new home.

One of the features I was originally drawn to was the rough-cut stone that formed fireplaces and walls in many of the rooms in the house. I knew that the stone was quarried on site and that sculptor Tony Smith, then just twenty-seven years of age, had worked on laying the horizontal courses during the original construction. There is a photograph taken during construction where the bearded young man is seated on top of the unfinished stone wall in the kitchen, looking very dapper in a dark fedora and with an overcoat draped over his shoulders. As I admired the character of the irregular shapes and the variation in color and size in the stone, I began to notice what appeared to be little abstract figures embedded naturally in the surfaces of their facets. Was that a little orange fox running toward the Point Room at eye level? A heron in flight on the tall wall of the kitchen? Snakes in battle in the children's dormitory? I wondered if Tony Smith had noticed the peculiarities of the stone and placed them for the Gunnings to discover. When I next saw Nora, I asked her about them. "Oh, you found them!" she exclaimed in delight.

After the movers came, we made haste in setting up our bed in the main bedroom and then worked our way to the kids' bedrooms. How wonderful it was to wake up to the view. The stone patio outside the bedroom dropped off so quickly it was like living high in the trees. Every day, we were witnesses to the rebirth of spring! Some mornings the sky filled with brilliant pinks behind the silhouette of the tower and the trees as the sun rose, while other days had a dull gray cast as the vernal rains fed the landscape, helping the buds pop from the tips of the branches.

Up in the treetops were clusters of dried leaves—squirrel nests perched high above the ground. After days passed, we were soon treated to the playful chasing of baby squirrels as they spiraled up and down the trees in pursuit of each other. It wasn't long before they mastered death-defying leaps to the thinnest of limbs, and despite the improbability of the maneuver, they always managed to handle the daring feat. When high winds would sway the treetops, shifting their nest from side to side, I wondered how the babies would fare. "They've been making their nests in treetops for eons," Joe would remind me. "They'll be fine."

Before the leaves reappeared, the nightly rising of planets in the eastern skies were a treat as they ascended in their orbits. Some nights, when there were clear skies, the moon would shine in, casting shadows of branches on the walls as it rose through the trees. Full moons were especially dramatic, starting as a huge orb close to the horizon and then rising to illuminate the grounds as they ascended in their orbits. When high in the night sky, the moon would shine through the skylights, illuminating its path on the floor below.

Living in a typical house, such as the home we lived in while restoring Glenbrow, you miss the connection with nature that we now enjoyed. Normally, you may take notice of extremes such as a rainstorm or high winds, but the subtle daily changes are hardly noticeable. Here, waking up every morning was a little different from the previous day. New growth and the reemergence of leaves changed the view from the day before, and it wasn't long before the homes on the opposite side of the ravine were blocked by the canopy of trees, filling the windows with a rich green. On days with a heavy rainfall, the creek would swell with a force of water that roared. Even with the windows closed, the loud rush could be heard throughout the house as the once docile creek churned in cascading whitewater rapids that overflowed the banks to extend all the way to the edges of the slope.

Besides adding beauty to the property, the vibrant flora also bestows nutritional benefits in a bounty of edible plants. My first discovery were fields of coveted ramps scattered along the edge of the creek. In early spring, the broad double-leafed plant is one of the first to emerge with its distinctive onion smell. Their popularity in recent years has caused an overharvesting of the plant that takes seven years to mature in order to produce seed. I adopted the sustainable harvest practice of leaving the bulb and only harvesting one of the leaves, of only about 15 percent of the entire crop. Whether sautéed with garlic and olive oil or made into a pesto, the flavorful plant is not only delicious but rich in vitamins A and C, selenium, and chromium.

Around the same time as ramps emerge, so do the much sought-after but more elusive morel mushrooms. With a spongy, brain-like appearance at the tip and a smooth, hollow cream-colored stalk, the mushrooms seem to pop out of nowhere from beneath piles of decaying leaves near certain deciduous trees. There is much folklore connected to foraging for morels: when the mayapples start to flatten; when dandelions begin to go to seed; when oak leaves are the size of squirrel ears; when ground temperatures hit fifty degrees, then start looking near decaying trees, especially ashes and elms. Both the morel and ramp season are short-lived, and both provide a nice reason to wander along the hillside in the springtime, learning about the native plants of the region.

We weren't the only ones mesmerized by the ravine. Lola Bola enjoyed the view she commanded when perched high above the creek in the Point Room. Her nemesis was a slow, laboring groundhog that lived in a hole just beyond the septic system lid. The animal's daily emergence would be met by the raucous baritone bark of the riled Labrador-Australian shepherd mix. The groundhog would acknowledge the noise, figure out that the pup was no threat, and so continue along its way. That changed after my friend Sarah visited and the screen door we had exited from in the kitchen didn't catch. After Sarah left, I was folding laundry in my bedroom when I thought I heard the muffled sound of Lola's bark, but it sounded somewhat distant. As I searched for her in the house, I discovered the open kitchen screen door. Her bark drew me to the dining room view of the ravine, where I caught her frantically digging just beyond the lid. I quickly donned my rain boots, grabbed a piece of leftover chicken from the refrigerator, and snatched her leash as I quickly headed around the outside corner of the western bedroom. "Bola, want a piece of chicken?" I called out, hoping the temptation of food would entice her away from the animal den. Bola looked up unfazed before resuming her digging, her dirty snout plunging deep into the hole. I quietly made my way down the steep incline, but just as I came within reach, she took off down the hill, running along the banks of the creek and heading downstream.

"Bola, come!" I called, "Want a piece of chicken?" I headed downstream in the direction she ran. Walking the bedrock bottom was tricky, with some of the rocks covered by a slippery mossy coating. The banks, on the other hand, had fallen branches, honeysuckle vines, and the chance of poison ivy to contend with as I made my way along the creek, occasionally calling her name. As I came around a bend, I saw her along a steep embankment, below striated layers of slate, digging in between a cluster of rocks. "Bola . . . yum! Chicken!" I called out as I approached her. She looked up, her nose covered with dirt before returning to the dig. As I got closer, her tail wagged and she turned toward me, "Chicken!" I offered, extending my arm. She headed right for me, but just before I could grab her, she brushed by me, running toward home.

I turned, both frustrated and angry. As I made my way back toward home, calling her name, she would occasionally come charging as if heading toward me only to keep going when I was about to grab her. Although frustrating for me, I realized it was a fun game for her. "Bye, Bola. Have a nice life!" I called as I headed up the hill toward home. Ascending the hill, I felt another brush against my pant leg as she whizzed by me, heading back to the creek. Tired, she laid down in the stream, lapping up the cool water while panting heavily in between drinks. I kept going uphill, knowing I needed to prepare for an outdoor dog bath. "You can move in with your groundhog friend. I'm going home," I called out to her. I went inside, grabbing the dog shampoo and a large beach towel. When I opened the door, there was Lola Bola, filthy dirty and panting rapidly from her adventure. "You are getting a bath with well water and it's freezing cold," I scolded her, grabbing her collar, hooking up the leash, and guiding her up to the hose that was attached to the well spout. The water was warm at first, the black hose heated by the sunlight, but soon the water was bone-chillingly cold as I sprayed away her layers of dirt. "This is what you get for not listening!" I told her. She slept like a baby the rest of the afternoon.

This wasn't the last of Bola's puppy adventures, despite my constant reminder to the kids to make sure the doors were closed. Lola Bola soon got the nickname "Bolting Bola," as she waited for any opportunity for an escape to freely roam the ravine. If it wasn't for a fear of her chasing an animal out to the rushing cars on Broad Street, I wouldn't have minded so much. Giving her an outdoor bath, however, wasn't the most enjoyable task, as her shaking often caused the one administering the bath to end up as wet as her.

One particular time, I was home alone when she spotted an opportunity to escape. After spending over a half hour trying to retrieve her as she headed toward the road, I called Joe at work. "I've been down by the creek trying to catch her for a half hour. There was a deer earlier, and I'm afraid if she sees it, she will chase it out to the road," I told him. "That's our Bolting Bola! I'll come home and help," Joe replied. After a while, I saw Joe come around the corner of the house. "Go get a piece of cheese to try to entice her," I called out. As Joe disappeared, I called out, "Bola! Your daddy's home!" knowing how excited she would get whenever Joe returned home. I soon heard the galloping of her paws racing through the water and then up the hill toward the house. She stopped at a large fallen ash tree, then proceeded up the hill in search of Joe. All of a sudden I heard Joe let out a loud screech. Bola had stopped to pick up the dead groundhog that she had finally caught and had laid it at Joe's feet.

The first major landscape project I would tackle after getting situated after the move would be returning to the zen garden, which had become the bane of my existence since its disturbance by the workmen. The area outside our bedroom had been disrupted by the masons' rebuilding of the stone retaining wall along the walkway. This garden was surrounded by a stacked stone wall that curved around the submerged area in a horseshoe shape that began parallel to the walkway steps and ended near the edge of the ravine. The wall framed a planter filled with ground cover known as yellow archangel—a member of the mint family with silvery green foliage and a butter-yellow flower that appears on stalks several inches tall. There was a sprinkling of peonies, columbine, and barrenwort mixed in as well. On the sunken ground level, I left a border of hostas that had been buried under the thick thistle and ivy along the eastern border. New landscape fabric was pinned around the edges with the exception of a small oval section around the stacked boulder focal point to allow some ground cover and a hosta to add color and texture.

The focal point of the garden is two stacked boulders, one a flattened blackish wedge anchored at about a thirty-degree angle to the top of an egg-shaped boulder in dappled shades of pink, brown, and gold. Surrounding the pair would be smooth, shiny, charcoal-colored Mexican river stones that I hand-selected from a local stone supplier to create an elliptical shape around the stacked boulders. Tiny cream-colored river pebbles would fill the sides of the sinuous horseshoe to the edge of the flagstone patio.

The planter was magnificent in mid-spring with its yellow flowers blooming, but I decided to add rhododendrons intermixed with azaleas in the beds to add more color, height, and texture. Their bright magenta cluster of flowers in early June would be followed by the lilac color of hostas and the pink blossoms of tall phlox by July. Our clay pots, moved from our former residences, would provide a mixture of colors and leaf forms with coleus, dianthus, geraniums, and impatiens. This ensured the steps of the walkway would always catch the eye and be a source of attraction to the honeybees that called our property home.

Working outside our bedroom in the zen garden, I began to notice the interesting contrast between the low horizontal house as it hugged the ground along edge of the ravine and the steep vertical tower backed up against the tall tree line. I knew from Mary Gunning's eulogy that Ted van Fossen had accompanied Rob and Mary Gunning, helping them to select the site for the house. "When we came to the land where we are all gathered," he said during the eulogy, "there was no question in my mind. Their house would be designed to marry the open field with the wooded ravine along the complete break that existed between them." Although he mainly worked on furniture and cabinetry in the original 1940 house, his choice of the site, as well as his contributions to the 1960s bedroom addition and tower demonstrated the important influence that Frank Lloyd Wright's principles of organic architecture had played in his life. Aged nineteen in 1940, the young man possessed a great sense understanding about how to site a building to best take advantage of the views as well as its environmental advantages.

Ted van Fossen,
Larry Cuneo
and Tony Smith
designing Glenbrow
in 1940.

*(photo courtesy the
Gunning family and Tony
Smith estate)*

Tony Smith sitting
atop stone wall during
1940 construction of
Glenbrow.

*(photo courtesy the Gunning
family and Tony Smith
estate)*

1940's view of the
house from the
ravine.

*(photo courtesy the
Gunning family)*

1964 Glenbrow tower
designed by Ted van
Fossen.

*(photo courtesy the Gunning
family)*

Front of Glenbrow as discovered in September 2013.

(photo by Maren Kuspan)

Kitchen patio with collapsed retaining wall, 2013.

(photo by Maren Kuspan)

Covered walkway in ruin with encroaching vines, 2013.

(photo by Maren Kuspan)

Laminate kitchen cabinetry as discovered in 2013.

(photo by Maren Kuspan)

View from kitchen with roof structure removed, 2014.

(photo by Dorri Steinhoff)

Concrete floor removed to install hydronic heat system and new plumbing, February 2015.

(photo by Joe Kuspan)

New concrete floor poured with original gridded imprint after installation of heating and plumbing, January 2016.

(photo by Joe Kuspan)

Stone Masons rebuild deteriorated stone planter on ravine facade of house, 2015.

(photo by Dorri Steinhoff)

Zen Garden and new walkway and studio, 2017.

(photo by Dorri Steinhoff)

Kitchen and dining room restored, 2018.

(photo by Maren Kuspan)

Restored living room with original built-in sofa, 2018.

(photo by Dorri Steinhoff)

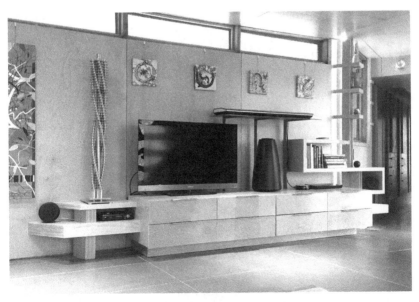

Custom AV cabinetry designed and fabricated by Joe Kuspan in living room with walk-in closet to far right, 2018.

(photo by Dorri Steinhoff)

CHAPTER 14:
Showcasing Glenbrow

That spring, I received an email from Becky West informing me that Ed Lentz had retired and she was now the executive director of the Columbus Landmarks Foundation. She was in the process of organizing a tour with Rush Creek Village, the community of about fifty Usonian-style homes that Ted van Fossen had designed in Worthington from the 1950s to the 1970s and was wondering if we would be interested in hosting a tour of Glenbrow on the same date. Since Glenbrow was on Columbus Landmarks' inaugural List of Most Endangered Buildings, they wanted to showcase a success in how a dilapidated property could be returned to its former glory.

She asked that we meet for coffee to discuss the plans, suggesting a meeting place near their office. At the coffee shop, I was pleased to see she brought her new associate with her, Nicole Devere. Nicole had lived in the apartments above my store in the Short North and had married our store leasing agent, Don, who had worked for developer Sandy Woods. (Don was now a local developer of historic properties as well as a Columbus Landmarks board member.) It was great to see them, especially Nicole, after almost twenty years! Their enthusiasm was contagious, and I enjoyed organizing this event with them. They had set a date in August for the Rush Creek Tour, and knowing Joe was working on cabinet fronts for the kitchen, I didn't think that time frame could be met. On top of all the tasks needing completion, we had scheduled a museum and restaurant trip to New York in July in part to see the *Frank Lloyd Wright at 150* show at MoMA; we felt the time frame for

August just didn't allow enough time. I invited them over to see the house, suggesting they wear comfortable shoes and telling them I would discuss a realistic date with Joe so we weren't overwhelmed with pressure.

Just before leaving for New York, Becky and Nicole came for their initial tour. "This is incredible, Dorri! I can't believe the amount of work you guys did in restoring Glenbrow," exclaimed Becky. "Believe me, there were times I thought we got in over our heads. Once you start a project like this, however, there is no turning back," I told her. "Our biggest challenge that caused the most stress was due to banks not allowing us to borrow against the equity we had put into the project in the final year to allow us to finish. It wasn't until the final six months that some small-town bank in Bucyrus, Ohio, lent us the funds to finish." "Well, you guys did an amazing job!" Nicole replied.

I suggested a date in October that would allow Landmark members to enjoy the colorful fall foliage while giving us the time we needed to finish up a couple of projects. Becky thought that would work out great and proposed a two-part event. "The first will be an informal talk/slide presentation to provide some history and context to the actual tour, and second would be a tour of the house. I am only going to open this event to Columbus Landmarks members. How many do you think we can accommodate?" Becky inquired. Since our parking situation wouldn't accommodate numerous cars, a bus could bring members to and from the house. Dave Vottero, the preservation architect who had advocated for the house and was a Columbus Landmarks board member, would serve with Joe on the inside tour while I would present the history and landscape outside. We decided to limit attendance to fifty Columbus Landmarks members besides the ancillary personnel. The tour sold out almost immediately.

We worked on projects in preparation, with Joe focused on cabinet doors while I worked on landscape maintenance. In July, following our NYC trip, where we were inspired by the High Line, Joe came up with a plan to create a long semicircle in a sequence of different plants, extending from the carport walkway to the stone cluster outside the western bedroom that we could admire as they changed with the seasons. Both of us were fans of Piet Oudolf's visionary planting designs, in how the skeletons of the summer perennials held an equal but different beauty in the fall and winter. We hoped to create a multi-season garden that could be enjoyed throughout the year, while protecting against snow drifting down to the submerged areas in the winter. Although this was a huge undertaking, we both couldn't wait to get started.

To our surprise, during our four-day absence in New York, Maren had removed the crumbling stone sides of the frog pond outside the front entrance, replaced the broken pieces, and then restacked them. Upon our return, Joe helped her move some larger broken limestone remnants of the outdoor tables that once were outside the front entrance of both the house and tower, creating two benches near the pond.

I started adding new plants in what would become our semicircular garden, beginning just beyond the black locust near the covered walkway, with new plantings extending for the length of the house from the carport studio to the western bedroom. Rhododendrons, azaleas, several different types of evergreens, and perennials were added to the Japanese maples, original to the site, that I had rescued from beneath encroaching vines. Knowing the woods along the ravine mainly featured yellow leaves in the fall, I decided to add more plants that would feature autumn reds and oranges. I added several more red osier dogwoods, whose red bark stood out in contrast to the white snow in winter, and that seemed to thrive in our soil. We had admired the smoke bushes at the High Line, so when I found some on sale at a garden store, I purchased both aubergine-colored and yellow-green-leafed bushes. I also focused on adding several perennials, organizing them in clusters of three to add a continuous bloom throughout the growing season, paying attention to how the plants would appear in the off-season as well.

As the heat of the summer faded to cooler temperatures, and with the house closer to completion, we resumed hosting dinner parties. Several architectural professors that were friends were among the first, followed by the PBS filmmaker, Dan, and his wife, Heather, along with Nora Gunning Chalfont, the eldest child of Rob and Mary Gunning. Dan wanted the opportunity to interview Nora about growing up in the house. What better way to discuss the history of the house and hear selected stories but over food and drink? Dave Vottero, the preservation architect who had advocated for the property prior to our purchase, and his wife, Lisa, also came for dinner. This would be Dave's first chance to experience the house since his 2009 tour with Kiki Smith, Seton Smith, and Sarah Auld, when the house was vacant. He had not visited the property since our purchase, so this would let him get reacquainted with the layout and our restoration.

I had been in regular contact with Sarah Auld, the executive director of the Tony Smith estate, providing updates on our construction progress and inviting her to the Landmarks tour. She was working with an art historian, Eileen Costello, on a *catalogue raisonné* of Tony Smith's architectural projects, with Glenbrow being his first built home. The tour provided them an opportunity to visit the house in person and experience its rebirth. We planned another dinner the evening after the tour to provide Dan the opportunity to interview Sarah and Eileen during their visit. I had worried that our use of birch plywood panels instead of the original Douglas fir would bother them. I explained that we salvaged all of the originals that we could, but when we needed replacements, we couldn't source Douglas fir with a similar quality of grain, so we purchased the closest match—birch. "That's exactly what Tony would have done! Work with what was available to him," Sarah explained, giving me a sense of relief.

The Landmarks tour was divided into segments on two consecutive weeks. First, there was an informal talk and slideshow presentation held at an architecture firm downtown, followed by the actual tour the following week. We selected photographs from the over 500 that had been taken during the course of construction, whittling the four years down into approximately an hour-and-a-half talk. Joe decided to use a photograph he'd taken from a cab window on a recent business trip to New Orleans to open the PowerPoint. It was a sign in front of a monument restoration in a park reading "Monumental Task Committee"! Joe is comfortable with public speaking, having presented to hospital boards, review boards, and clients his entire career, but for me, not having given a talk before a large group since a Toastmaster club in graduate school, I was starting to feel some butterflies. We started off with me presenting the history of house and the people involved in its creation, followed by Joe describing the process of our restoration, with both of us contributing anecdotes about the journey. The talk was well-attended and received. Afterward, Becky and Nicole were full of praise and suggested that we should take the talk on the road. "The only road we are interested in is our own, so we can work on getting the house ready for the tour!" we joked.

Preparing to open your house to dozens of strangers is somewhat nerve-racking at any time, but hosting an event full of architects, preservationists, and people involved in the arts makes for added stress. Having the kids away at college made it slightly easier because their rooms could be prepared ahead of time, but still, there was a myriad of chores to attend to before the big day. I made arrangements for Lola Bola to spend the night at a local doggie daycare facility, but with Whisper's advanced age, confusion, and diminishing senses, I knew the experience would be too much. I recruited Fia, asking her to break away from her architecture studio time to babysit sixteen-year-old Whisper during the day of the tour. Becky and Nicole organized the food and drink, along with bus transportation from the Landmarks' office to the house. Our daunting task was to prepare the property as best we could despite the long to-do list hanging over our heads.

The small area along the stepping-stones in the lower courtyard in front of the house had been full of weeds, but after digging it out, I planted a variety of different sedum mixed with some small, football-sized, smooth rocks that Joe had recovered from a construction site near his office. The week before the tour, I scoured local garden stores to find a few plants still in bloom to replace some that were in decline in the clay pots along the walkway.

Although many of the stores had removed most of the plants for the season, I found a great array of geraniums, in a variety of colors and leaf shape, along with several seasonal ornamental cabbages to fill in some of the empty spaces. I also discovered that the garden store up the street had the best-shaped large pumpkins with long, thick, twisted stems protruding from their tops. I bought several tall, oblong pumpkins along with some colorful ornamental squashes, with protruding hooks and bumpy textures, to mix with multicolored dried corncobs in a festive display to celebrate the autumn season, as well as to serve as a barricade to paver stones in need of relaying.

The Sunday afternoon of the tour was a warm sunny day—perfect weather with almost optimal fall color. Late blooming coneflowers, autumn-fire tall sedum, and autumn crocuses intermixed with the newly planted bushes to set up a pop of color in the front of the house, in contrast to the changing yellow foliage of the background. The pots along the walkway were filled with a variety of mature coleus with their variegated leaves, the newly added geraniums, and remnants of the deep orange and magenta impatiens from earlier in the season.

I set up a trifold posterboard on an easel with historic and "before" photographs so I could inform attendees of just how ambitious the transformation was. The caterers were the first to arrive, followed by Dan, the filmmaker following our journey, with his collection of cameras and lenses. Sarah and Eileen arrived shortly before the bus. After years of email correspondence, it was nice to finally meet Sarah in person. They would be joining us along with Dan for dinner afterward to allow time for filming an interview. With so many experts in attendance, it was slightly intimidating to present a history of the house and those who designed it, but after my years of research, I knew it as well as anyone.

The tour bus parked at the end of the driveway and Dave Vottero was the first to exit. He rode with the bus to provide history and background to attendees en route. Closely following him were architecture-lovers who were eager to see the results of our efforts. Among the guests of honor were

Executive Director Sarah Auld and art historian Eileen Costello from the
Tony Smith Foundation, who briefly provided background. The poet, Rikki
Santer, recited her poem, "Readability of Place, Blacklick, OH," and Albert
van Fossen, the ninety-four-year-old brother of Ted, provided background on
the young designers, including how astonished he was in meeting Tony while
visiting the house under construction, who "was the first man he had ever met
with a beard!" Becky read a moving letter that Mary Gunning had written to
Tony Smith in January of 1941, expressing her gratitude:

> It is such a beautiful house and living in it is so good. I feel a debt
> to you and Ted all my life long. I never get through with the joy
> of looking and there is always a quiet and a peace and yet a deep
> excitement. . . . You must know that it is your home too—and for Ted
> too. I think the making of something like this home is something that
> belongs to you so close that it will never be lost. It will be here waiting
> and there are plenty of beds in the dormitory. . . . Give my regards to
> Ted and tell him those parts of the house where books are kept and
> where we sit and work and keep things are really beautiful.

We divided the fifty Landmarks members into two groups, with half
to be inside, while the other half remained outdoors with me. Those inside
divided again to be led by either Joe or Dave, each in their own section of
the house so that the rooms would never get overcrowded. Dave took his
half inside, covering the kitchen, dining room, and western bedroom, while
the other half toured the Point Room, living room, and bedroom with Joe.
They described our correcting of design flaws and attempting to stay true
to the original layout, but with the knowledge that this was not a museum,
but a house restored for a family in the twenty-first century. Joe highlighted
projects for his near future, including built-in furniture for our television and
stereo, a computer station for below the bookshelves in the living room, and
a dining room table that could seat eight.

Outside, I used the poster with photographs to provide some history about the house, showing its dilapidated condition when we discovered it, the Gunning family, and the designers, and then I guided folks on a tour of the property, highlighting the exterior of the tower, the studio/carport, the covered walkway, and of course, the main house. I discussed how the three young designers had met at the New Bauhaus in Chicago and later worked on houses for Frank Lloyd Wright, adopting his principles of organic architecture. Wright had taught them the importance of a site plan, "No house should be on a hill or on anything. It should be of the hill. Belonging to it. Hill and house should live together each the happier for the other," he had instructed.

I explained the genius of their site plan, which orientated the house to take advantage of the cool breezes of the prevailing wind during the warm months and also provided protection from the bitter north winds with a wall of tall spruces in the winter. The windows and doors along the ravine were oriented to the south, the sun warming the house when the foliage had dropped off the trees, while those same trees provided shade from the blazing summer sun. "We noticed on the summer solstice that the setting western sun travels through the opening to the tennis court and through the window between the living room and eastern bedroom and out the French doors, out to the sculpture garden," I informed them. "We also noticed, that in the winter with the leaves fallen, the Point Room, originally Rob and Mary's bedroom, enjoys the sun's rays from sunrise to sunset."

I took them to the pond, explaining that the Gunnings had a built-in pool that had been filled in by the previous owner. "I can't imagine swimming in a pool here, seeing how many two- to three-foot water snakes we have. But I believe the Gunning children were more adventurous than I am! Nora has told us how as a child she would pick up the snakes and wrap them around her shoulders like a feathered boa!" I explained to the gasps of some. "I appreciate they are part of the ecosystem and they keep down the rodent population, but I have no interest in handling them. They usually rest on those partially submerged rocks in the water on the far side of the pond, although occasionally I will find one while weeding, coiled under the yucca plants. You can tell they are digesting, with a thick bulge in their midsection with peristaltic waves assisting the process."

I explained that the second owners, the Neuenschwanders, had added the pond, built up the earth along the road as a buffer, and then added the boulders that cascaded along the edges. "In exploring the far side of the pond, we discovered some pipes and an electrical line, leading us to believe there was once a waterfall on the opposite side. We want to recreate the waterfall, but first we need to tackle a massive amount of poison ivy that's growing over there," I explained. "We are hoping the flow of water will help filter some of the street noise and add water circulation to the manmade pond." They were also responsible for the canal stone wall and the interesting protruding stone pieces near the pond. "I always thought that someday it would be cool to use the elevated land formed by the canal stones as a stage for a band to play, but until then, they make a comfortable bench to rest on. They also added landscaping behind the berm: yews, evergreen trees, and grasses now dwarfed by natural propagation.

At the tennis court, I pointed out how the trees, some now over twenty feet tall, grew up through the painted lines of the court, breaking through the asphalt topping, creating shade for what we now used as a patio. "When we discovered the property, there were large branches that had broken off the black locust tree, laying on the court, and covered in honeysuckle, grapevine, and poison ivy. Maren and I worked at clearing off the overgrowth and discovered this bed of sedum surviving on the hard surface of the court. Covering about a quarter of the south end of the court, it blooms a brilliant yellow in late spring. Being drought resistant, it's perfect for the impervious surface of the court." I also described how for the first year, we used a bushwhacker to trim the edges but had since allowed them to revert back to prairie, explaining our concept for planting a multi-seasonal landscape, keeping the natural growth of prairie and woodlands with minimal disturbance to the wildlife. "I've always loved Queen Anne's lace, with their dainty, tiny white flowers and feathery leaves during the summer, and this time of year, the goldenrod and asters provide not only beauty but food for the honeybees, butterflies, and birds."

I pointed out the tall cypress tree growing in the low area just beyond the court, abutting the fences behind the tract homes to the west: "The ground is low and floods with heavy rains, perfect for a tree that normally grows in swamps. To help hide the fences and suburban development, we wanted to plant fast-growing trees. Discovering that the metasequoia, also known as a dawn redwood—a close relative of the cypress that favored wet conditions and could grow five to seven feet per year—we thought it would be a perfect addition. In researching the tree, I learned that although it was indigenous to North America, they were thought to have gone extinct along with the dinosaurs. In 1941, a grove was discovered in the Sichuan region of China. Since 1941 was the year the Gunnings moved into their new house, we thought how appropriate it was for us to plant."

We traveled on a path through the Norway spruces that led to the yard west of the main house toward the firepit. "We discovered these boulders on the edge of the tennis court under invasive vines," I explained, while pointing to eight shin-high irregular rocks spread to form a circle. "When we had a front-end loader here to remove the accumulated stone and soil from the plumbers' excavation of the floors, I had them move and position the rocks so that we could have an area for a fire."

At the far side of the house, I pointed out a small deviation from Wright's Usonians. "We added galvanized steel, half-round gutters over the kitchen patio and the dining room wall of French doors, which spill water onto these rock piles, preventing the doors from constantly having water spots," I explained. "The patio outside the kitchen is below the natural ground level, so it used to fill with water during heavy rains. Diverting the water with a gutter and adding a linear drain beneath the edge of the retaining wall has corrected the problem." I encouraged them to take turns going around the stepping-stones to the back of the house to see the ravine. "When we purchased the property, the hillside was so full of vines that you couldn't see the creek. Now we enjoy the view year-round. The planter outside the dining room was added in part as a buffer to keep folks from stepping off the edge, whereas the cantilevered planter below the Point Room was completely restored to its original state and a new drain was added to prevent it from becoming waterlogged."

After viewing the ravine side of the house, we traveled down the steps to the kitchen patio. I pointed out how the retaining wall had collapsed, causing mud to travel down into the house. "We cheated! We had the stonemasons build a concrete-block retaining wall in front of the rebuilt stone wall so we never had to experience that again!" The concrete block was exposed in an area about four feet in width. "This area was left blank for a future wood-fired pizza oven. Joe built one for us at our Noverre Musson house and we used it all the time. "Beyond the exposed block was the gabion wall that I built. I explained how it was a partial solution to the giant mounds of aggregate that had been removed by the plumbers during construction from beneath the old concrete floor. The idea to introduce a gabion wall was borrowed from an outdoor garden we saw at the Cranbrook Science Museum. "There are seven cage bins," I explained, "Adam estimated that each bin holds approximately 1,100 pounds of rock. I carried all that rock in buckets from the upper lawn, and although you might think you just dump them in, the rocks needed to be wedged together individually. This was our way of incorporating some of the original stone that was unearthed in the replacement of the floor and hydronic heating system."

From the patio, we traveled around the front of the house to the zen garden, and I pointed out that new trench drains lay underneath the small river stone along the path. We gathered on the side of our bedroom so the entire sunken court could be viewed. "We didn't realize there were stacked boulders here when we first discovered the property. The weeds were that tall! Also, the patio along the house was buried under several inches of composted material. I was weeding with a dandelion tool when I hit the hard surface. I felt like an archeologist unearthing buried treasure upon discovering the limestone patio." The zen garden provided a nice view of the studio that overlooked it from elevated ground. "That studio was originally three small rooms, with one of them a seven-by-eight room called the Monk's Cell," the room where we had discovered the gold necklaces lost by Nora many years before. "Ted van Fossen lived in the unheated Monk's Cell after he returned to Columbus from California in the early 1950s." Although the low branches of the giant oak tree partially obscured the tower, the zen garden provided perhaps the best view of the building while foliage was still on the trees. "The tower was designed by Ted van Fossen in the early 1960s to be used by Mr. Gunning as an office with a guest suite above and a top-floor roof terrace with a Murphy bed. In the days before air-conditioning, sleeping porches were used during hot weather," I explained. "The ground level had been a workroom that housed a kiln for the Gunning's art projects, which, unfortunately, was stolen before our time."

Afterward we invited questions and allowed those on the tour to wander the grounds with the exception of the unsafe tower. We reiterated to our guests that our purpose was not a faithful restoration based on the 1940 plans and subsequent additions over the years, but to rebuild upon the original, using current practices, code requirements, and advances in construction technology, and using as much salvable original material as possible. "The extent of the damage when we purchased the property was a limiting factor, but we remained true to its ethic while acknowledging present-day lifestyles and incorporating current environmental and technical advances," Joe explained.

After the tour, we thanked Sarah and Eileen, who would be joining us for dinner later that evening. Dan set up cameras and lighting in the living room, using its horizontal windows framed by stone piers as a backdrop for after-dinner interviews as Joe and I prepared the food. It was an opportunity for him to record a noted expert on the biography of Tony Smith.

We took a minor hiatus from restoration work for a couple weeks until we were asked if we would host a house tour for the Columbus chapter of the American Institute of Architects (AIA). We agreed to an April tour, providing us with another deadline to spur us on to accomplish tasks during the cold winter months. Although we sound as if we are gluttons for punishment, these deadlines ensure that these necessary projects get completed in a timely manner.

Joe set goals to finish the living room's built-in furniture, including having cushions made for the original sofa, and Usonian-style shelving in the bathrooms. He had hoped to use birch plywood scraps from the house ceiling and wall panels, with only minimal purchases of new wood. He drew plans for the entertainment system cabinetry that would rest under the clerestory windows, using the original built-in closets and shelving that were once there as his inspiration. Starting the day after Christmas, my living room became a temporary workroom during the cold winter months. We had retained the steel shelf and stand from an earlier custom stereo cabinet, which were specifically fabricated for my vintage Bang and Olufsen stereo, so Joe designed around that component, extending it from a new low horizontal base in birch plywood that featured eight drawers for his collection of CDs and a place for the television. Using the same geometry as the original table and shelving that had extended off the closets, he recreated an abbreviated version in birch plywood that terminated the drawers at each end. At one end of the cabinet, he extended the line of shelving upward, snaking its way back and forth around a wood-mast element and terminating at the angled front corner of the living room. This vertical accent concealed recessed LED lighting and supported three tiny projecting shelves, marking the step down into the main bedroom.

CHAPTER 15:
Accolades

A heavy snowfall at Glenbrow is a magical time. The ravine, once a dull russet color of dried leaves, gets a blanket of white that defines the hillside and coats the tree branches. The thick trunks of once majestic ash trees, decimated by emerald ash borers, lay still in their final resting places extending down the hillside, a milky layer on top of their rippled bark. Snow covers clusters of rocks in the creek to form islands of white surrounded by the slow-moving, dark water, reflecting the overcast sky. The lofty Norway spruce trees look like a Christmas postcard with their tips covered in a dusting of snow. Before the footprints of dogs and boots can leave their mark, the smooth drifts of white look picture-perfect against the backdrop of the warm glow of lights inside the house. Long glistening icicles form below the galvanized gutters that run along the roofline on the western edge as water slowly drips down to the rock piles below. The scene is even more enjoyable when viewed from within the warm confines of the house while holding a cup of steaming tea. Still, as the cold, gray days linger, especially after a few times shoveling and maneuvering across the slick ice, I'm counting the days until spring.

The cold weather is the perfect excuse to focus on inside projects. We couldn't wait to have the built-in sofa completed. The house had a custom mattress made for the sofa, but to save money, we opted for three custom cushions with removable covers on a single foam pad covered in a muslin fabric. This would allow the sofa to be used for sleeping on the cushions in case we needed an additional bed for a guest. We chose a warm, stone-gray colored upholstery for the cushions and decided to use pillows for brighter accent colors. Our palette was inspired by the moss that grew between the stones of the patio outside our bedroom and featured a lichen green, mustard gold, and a broad range of warm gray tones. One day, Karen Rumora, one of our artist friends, posted photographs of a series of handmade pillows she made as an extension of her "Biophilia" series. They incorporated rich natural tones in an impressionist landscape that Karen had printed on canvas. I purchased three of the pillows that looked perfect against the cushions and stone wall behind the sofa. We also purchased an abstract wool rug in the same tones for the living room floor. The room was starting to look finished!

Late in February, the emerging snowdrops mark the first hint of spring, and with days growing longer, there's anticipation of warmer weather. It would be at least another month before the daffodils would begin popping above the ground and even longer for the early forsythia to bloom. Still, on warm days, we set to work to prepare the yard for the upcoming spring tour, raking the remaining leaves, clearing old growth of the perennials, and trimming away the dried strands of ornamental grasses from the previous year.

Joe worked on extending the edge of the arcing landscape element he had started the previous fall, using the garden hose as a guide for the gently curved edge. I continued to fill the freshly excavated garden bed with perennials to fill in the new boundary he created. During this time, we heard from Becky West that we had been named Columbus Landmarks' "Outstanding Persons of the Year" for Glenbrow's restoration—a nice and welcomed acknowledgement for our hard work. She also presented us with Cross pens, suggesting that after our presentation went so well, I should think about writing my memoirs of all our rich stories, planting the seed for the future!

The late April day of the AIA tour was overcast, but rain had held off for the tour. There was no need to prepare the presentation material because several mini-tours had occurred since last autumn and the words seemed to flow without thought. Many of those in attendance, being architects, had visited the site in its ruined state and offered kind words for our work. Jim Weiker, a reporter for the *Columbus Dispatch*, who had written about our undertaking back in 2014, was in attendance and interviewed some of the architects, opening his subsequent article by calling Glenbrow "the most important modern house in Central Ohio." We had little knowledge of how important our property was viewed when we first discovered it, but now we had come to realize how beloved the house was within the community. When friends would speak of our selfless and heroic undertaking, we would laugh, knowing the truly selfish motives behind the purchase!

Late that summer, we were notified by the State of Ohio Historic Preservation Office that our restoration was to receive a merit award for the preservation of the Gunning House. I also received state approval to proceed to the National Register of Historic Places, but I decided to wait until the completion of the tower so the entire property would be recognized.

CHAPTER 16:
Uncomfortable Creature Comforts

The school year ended with the kids moving into Glenbrow. Fia only stayed for a day before leaving for Europe to study abroad in Rome for the summer and then spending a couple weeks traveling with friends before classes started. Maren graduated from architecture school and by May had moved back into the house in time to enjoy the brilliance of spring.

Having spent her final fall semester in a design/build program in the historic Over-the-Rhine district of Cincinnati, Maren had developed an interest in preserving historic buildings. That interest led to her interviewing over the winter break at Schooley Caldwell, a firm that specialized in preservation and adaptive reuse. She had returned to school early after New Year's Day of her final year to take a five-day-a-week concentrated course offered during the entire month of January when most students had not returned for the semester. With winter weather and few friends on campus, she focused her downtime on a design competition that a friend had informed her about. The competition was to design a building on an empty lot in the Over-The-Rhine neighborhood that the local historic foundation could use as a prototype to show developers. Since the class she was taking was not challenging, and she had a lot of time on her hands, Maren focused on the competition. There were only two student entries in the competition, and most of those competing were individual registered architects or teams from architecture firms. Just before her graduation, we learned Maren's design won second place in the competition with a welcomed award of $1,000 to compensate her for her efforts! It was a great accomplishment to add to her resume and portfolio as well.

Maren's first Sunday back home was a warm sunny day, and we opened up the house to enjoy the breeze and the sounds of nature. *Jazz Sunday* was on the radio as I cut vegetables for a salad. Lola Bola, off in the Point Room scoping the terrain for wildlife, started sounding an unusual bark, not her usual baritone howl upon spotting movement in the ravine. As it continued, I stopped to see what had caught her attention. She was hunched over, with her focus directed at the corner of the point, and following her nose, I spotted a black snake coiled in the corner. "Oh my God! Joe, quick, there's a snake in the Point Room!" I screamed. Both Maren and Joe appeared, as I grabbed the dog and ordered Maren to go up to the carport and grab the trash-picker tool. "I warned you before that I could see light coming through at the point!" I had noticed we were missing the cypress trim piece that enclosed the corner of the point on the exterior, an inadvertent omission during construction. "You kept telling me you'd get to it. Thank God Fia wasn't here!"

Maren quickly returned and handed the tool to Joe. We opened one of the French doors and Joe gingerly picked up the snake with the prongs of the tool, releasing it outside, where it quickly disappeared into the brush. "You have got to search this room and her bathroom and make sure there are no others. Fia would absolutely freak out!" I went back to cutting vegetables, leaving Joe to search. Returning to check on him after a few minutes, I discovered him near the entrance to the bathroom holding a two-foot-long molted snakeskin. "Did you place this on the stone wall?" he asked me. "Are you serious? You really think I would move a snakeskin to Fia's bedroom?" I replied back. "You need to get a ladder and search the bathroom's nooks and crannies looking for more. And you better seal the crack so we don't get any other visitors!" No more snakes were found, and Joe finally caulked the crack until the missing cypress trim could seal it for good.

Besides planting a few more perennials, we finally got to celebrate our hard work while enjoying happy hour out on the tennis court under the shade of the trees. Having cleared out the raspberry bramble and honeysuckle that were growing in the sedum that covered over a quarter of the court on the south end, we could now enjoy the low bed of bright yellow flowers in late spring, abuzz with honeybees. Drought-resistant sedum would fade to a dull green in dry weather but would pop back to life after a rain. The flat green hardscape of the former tennis court provided the perfect place to set up our teak dining table with its umbrella that provided extra protection against the sun as it filtered through the leaves of a mature black locust in the later afternoon—the perfect spot to enjoy a good book and a glass of wine with a pup or two at your feet.

CHAPTER 17:

Quest for an Ivory Tower

A late summer torrential downpour drew our attention back to phase 2—the tower. We had found the 1964 building by Ted van Fossen to be in even worse shape than the house, and shortly after purchasing the property, we hired a contractor to remediate the mold and remove the affected black, soggy drywall. Joe had determined that there were extensive design flaws in the roof and roof terrace that did not allow rainwater to properly drain from the roof. The drywall removal had exposed vulnerable areas that Joe needed to address, and he attempted to use tar paper to temporarily patch the areas where water was entering until we were ready to properly tackle that job. Unfortunately, this still allowed some water to penetrate, and we knew the roof needed a complete replacement, not merely patches.

There were two different roofs on the tower to replace—the upper roof above the stairwell and the roof terrace, both with major issues. With fall approaching, Joe decided that the two surfaces would need to be completed in two phases. Starting on the top, Joe designed a solution for a seven-sided, gently sloping roof cap above the staircase, while adding yet another temporary layer of felt paper to the corner of the terrace that continued to leak. Extending ladders from the roof terrace, he removed the rotted portions of the six-inch parapet walls and several inches of tar and gravel built-up roof, tossing the heavy pieces over the edge to near the zen garden entrance. This meant that he was working up on the tallest part of the tower. It seemed high, viewing him from the yard below, but when you consider the sides and rear along the ravine are on a very steep decline, it was absolutely nerve-racking! I pleaded with him to use a safety harness but to no avail. "You are going to be the death of me yet!" I told him. "I can't even watch! Make sure all your life insurance is up to date!" I joked.

His design consisted of constructing a new frame to create a low, slope-pitched roof that would slightly overhang the existing parapets to drain water over the edges and provide proper ventilation below the new EPDM membrane. In the cavity below the new frame, scrap pieces of tapered insulation from the house roof were placed and a deck of OSB sheathing was applied. He finished the upper framing while the weather was still nice but had to wait in the queue for the roofers. To keep the board dry, he draped a huge tarp over the top, dangling over the edges with weights attached to the tarp grommets. By early November, the roofers came and installed the roof membrane and its metal drip edges. After cleaning off the terrace of leaves, buckeyes, and acorns, Joe placed the tarp over the terrace, with bricks holding it in place, in preparation for the approaching winter. Another temporary solution until the warmer, drier weather of spring returned.

After the festivities of the holidays passed, cold weather usually blows in from the northwest with a biting wind that removes the last vestiges of foliage and needles from the swaying tree branches overhead. The weather seems to change abruptly, and the harsh winter temperatures keep outdoor activities to a minimum, when heavy boots and multiple layers of clothing are needed. Freshly fallen snow is beautiful as it coats the boughs of the imposing Norway spruces, but it can also be a major nuisance for us to exit the property. The road, being a major east-west thoroughfare, receives frequent passes by snowplows followed by salt trucks. There are two lanes in each direction, a turning lane in between, plus paved berms that the mail carrier uses—all of which get plowed in front of the driveway, creating a mountain of snow to remove. Add salt to the equation and you get very heavy slush. If the temperatures get really cold overnight, the slush freezes into a block of ice. Forget those light, ergonomic, store-bought snow shovels! This calls for a heavy-duty coal shovel to hold the weight and to take the abuse of chipping away the ice! When you add a fifty-mile-per-hour speed limit to the mix (with testosterone-driven SUV drivers who think slowing down is for other people!), you get a dangerous situation. If only there was a fast-forward button to get through January and February!

At times, the creek becomes a block of ice with just a thin line of black water moving slowly beneath the frozen mass. On days when bright sunshine replaces the gray overcast skies, portions of the creek melt, leaving islands of white ice formed around groups of boulders with dark water glistening in between. When the night skies are clear with a bright moon overhead, the moonbeams reflect off the water and clusters of ice, creating a surrealistic otherworldly landscape. Nora warned us of the danger of ice dams after heavy precipitation as temperatures rise after an extended cold period. A seemingly tranquil frozen creek can become a dangerous raging river as melting ice can release a torrential flood in a matter of moments.

During the cold weather, the walkway steps can get icy and challenging after sundown, and we don't normally use melting products for fear of damage to the environment. With the unpredictable weather, we seldom invite others over during the winter months, instead feeling content with good books to read or binge-watching a television series. Winter 2019 brought the bitter cold of a polar vortex through the area, further limiting our time spent outside. I added felt strips in the cracks around windows and doors whenever I felt even the slightest draft. When the temperatures outside dropped below zero, temporary pop-in rods were used to install makeshift curtains over the single-pane beveled corner glass, the western bedroom corner window, and the double casement window between the living room and laundry room.

CHAPTER 18:
Unlikely Visitors

One of the wonderful surprises we didn't expect when restoring the house was the interesting people we would meet because of it. Besides the Gunning family, their extended family members, and people associated with preservation, there were others we would never have encountered if not for the restoration. One particularly frigid January day in the winter of 2019, after returning from grocery shopping, there was a knock on the door. The front entrance is so unusually placed that often, when friends come to the house for the first time, they don't know where to go, so a knock on the door was very unusual and unexpected, especially on such a frigid day. Not knowing who would brave single digit temperatures to visit, I ventured out the kitchen door, holding on to Lola Bola's collar for protection, just in case. Outside stood a well-dressed young man in a mid-waist, light leather jacket, no gloves, and dress shoes, obviously from a warmer climate. Andrew Romano told me he was a journalist who was in town to interview Senator Sherrod Brown about his possible run for the presidency. He had known about the house and apologized about the unexpected visit. I invited him into the kitchen, saying, "Only a die-hard architecture lover would brave this cold to visit an out-of-the-way building!" Andrew informed me that he owned R. M. Schindler's Walker House in Silverlake, a neighborhood in Los Angeles. "Schindler is one of my husband's favorite architects! We have several books on his works," I told him. Still, my house was a mess: "I hadn't put away the nonperishable groceries. They're still sitting on the island. I had just emptied the contents of my dryer on my bed for folding. I never feel comfortable in showing the house in this condition," I explained. "I understand. I'm picky about the condition I show my house in. Would you mind if I take some photos outside?" "Of course you are welcome to. Please contact me ahead of time next time you are in town and I will gladly provide a tour." We exchanged contact information and he invited me and Joe to visit his Walker House next time we were in Los Angeles. The following month, a book he wrote about the Walker House was released and we added it to our collection.

While we were awaiting warmer weather to return, I also received a request from our friend Jane Murphy, a professor at OSU's Knowlton School of Architecture, who recently had had dinner at our house. Jane conveyed that she had met with Jo-ey Tang, Director of Exhibitions at Beeler Gallery at Columbus College of Art and Design, along with a visual artist from Paris. Laëtitia Badaut Haussmann was a French artist who had previously mounted an exhibition at Maison Louis Carré in France, designed by Alvar Aalto. "She is interested in the mutability of a work of architecture over time, including the lives of those who live in it." Jane informed me that they had visited other sites in town, but, "I suspect that your house may be more interesting on many levels." Laëtitia was just in town until the end of the weekend, so despite the cold weather, we invited them over to tour the house.

Prior to their arrival, I researched Laëtitia's work to better understand why she might be interested in Glenbrow. She conceived a recent installation that used Aalto's Maison Louis Carrè, an important modernist house southwest of Paris that had been designed for a prominent art dealer, as a site. The installation was the third chapter from the artistic group, Laboratoire Artistique Du Groupe Bel, in a series exploring the connection between iconic modernist buildings and contemporary art. The previous two chapters had been site specific to the Barcelona Pavilion by Mies van der Rohe and Le Corbusier's Villa Savoye, near Paris. Maison Louis Carrè's website described her concept by stating, "Her works weave together both historical and fictive trajectories of people, places and objects, freely blending the influences of literature, cinema and design." "Wow! Just wow! And we were just waiting out the doldrums of winter!" I said to Joe. "We better get to an early spring cleaning," pointing to the line of winter boots, scarves, and hats that had gathered around the bench near the entrance due to the cold weather.

Besides using Maison Louis Carré as a setting for an exhibition, I also discovered she had previously participated in a 2018 group show with Kiki Smith, a well-known and respected visual artist who happened to be the daughter of Tony Smith, the original designer of Glenbrow. The group show had also featured Gerhard Richter, an artist we admired and who had been the focus of a documentary we had just watched entitled, *Gerhard Richter—Painting*.

Jo-ey likewise had an impressive background, with curatorial experience in Paris, New York, Prague, and Hong Kong before coming to Beeler Gallery. He was also an artist with an upcoming 2020 exhibit at the Centre Pompidou in Paris in conjunction with another artist, and he had also written reviews for art publications. It was quite a thrill for us art lovers from the Midwest to host this tour in the dead of winter, usually a time we see few visitors.

Jo-ey and Laëtitia arrived with Joseph, a colleague from Beeler Gallery, on a bright, sunny, although frigid, Saturday afternoon in early February. Laëtitia was tall with an elegant demeanor, with full red lips and silvery hair that was loosely pulled up with curls flowing down across her forehead. One focus of her work included historical references, and it was obvious that she took the time to research Glenbrow prior to her visit. Jo-ey had jet black, shoulder-length hair tucked behind his ears and dressed stylishly with a scarf wrapped around his neck against the cold. Like Laëtitia, he came well-informed and was sincerely inquisitive about the property.

After I offered a brief history of the house, Joe explained how the young designers had incorporated Wright's principles of organic architecture. "Wright emphasized the building should be in harmony with nature, that the building should grow out of the land. Be a part of it rather than simply placed on top of it. These young designers, fresh from the spell of Wright, took it quite literally—by inserting this building into the land just below ground level," Joe explained. "They also sought to connect the inside with the outside." Joe explained how he designs children's hospitals for a living and how the space within can create a healing environment. "We use natural light and views of nature to encourage a therapeutic response in the patient. Wright utilized these concepts years ago. This house is over seventy-five years old. At that time, most houses had small windows and little connection to the environment or their site. Wright was way ahead of his time," Joe explained. "This is a classic example of prospect and refuge. While the facade of the house that faces the road is enclosed and protects the occupants' privacy—as in refuge—the backside is glass, with views over the entire ravine, which provides prospect." Joe further explained that "the stone and wood are primitive and appealing to the oldest instincts of human beings." I explained, "This is a house designed for the well-being of its inhabitants. Despite the close proximity of suburbia, once you enter this property, you feel removed from the problems of the world. It's easy to forget the daily grind of the outside world and get lost in the moment—be it a frog basking in the sun, a new wildflower that just bloomed, or the wind whistling through the leaves," I added. After an abbreviated tour of the grounds due to the cold, we headed indoors and into the warmth.

Inside, I referred them to the foldout board I have used in the past that included both historic photographs and those of how Glenbrow looked when we discovered the property. "I've kept this board from previous tours with Landmarks and the AIA. It's easier to show the level of decay with photos than with words alone." With such a private tour, we could add details perhaps too esoteric for a larger group. "Our friend, Dave Vottero, provided a tour of the house when Kiki and Seton Smith came to town to advocate for the house back in 2009. Dave told us the story that when Kiki came into what is now our dining room, she could sense where the addition was added without even having it pointed out. She could feel a difference in the space that her father had designed and the later addition by Ted van Fossen," I informed them, while describing the different phases of additions to the house. Laëtitia told us she was planning to contact Kiki about including a piece of her work in an upcoming show in France she was working on. We pointed out how the early photos demonstrated how the entire wall of the room was continuous French doors, but that Ted van Fossen had interrupted that continuity to relocate a pair to the addition, replacing their original location with a large piece of plate glass. "What are French doors?" Laëtitia asked. "These pairs of doors with glass," I responded. "What do the French call them?" I asked. "Doors!" she replied back, as we all laughed.

Laëtitia appeared fascinated by a sculpture that Joe had collaborated on with his friend, Ralph Williams, to create. He pointed out the dresser with the built-in changing table depression and the bookshelf that used colored epoxy and steel tubes that Ralph had salvaged from the scrapyard, as well as the oak "Mother and Child" piece in the living room. Her eye was drawn to a piece Joe had commissioned for my fiftieth birthday. "This piece reminds me of Marina City in Chicago by Bertrand Goldberg," I explained. "I always think of Wilco's *Yankee Hotel Foxtrot* album cover—one of my favorite albums whenever I'm playing with our pup on the floor." Joe pointed out how "the helix has four rods, with fifty segments of hand-cut aluminum stacked vertically, each with a cut piece of aluminum between, except for three bronze pieces, representing the year we married, and the years of the birth of our children, Maren and Fia." I added, "Those aluminum segments remind me of shapes from Tony Smith paintings of the early 1950s." Laëtitia took many photos, with Joe providing animated commentary so our hour-long tour lasted closer to two hours.

As we walked them up the walkway, Joe asked if they wanted to see the tower. "Of course!" they replied. We explained that we had found it in even worse condition than the main house and it was currently gutted and sealed for winter. "This is my next project in the spring, after we return from a trip to Europe." Like the main house, the tower was brighter in winter with the surrounding trees bare for the season. There were still thick pieces of transparent plastic covering some of the broken windows, but the brilliant sunlight lit up the space, making it more inviting than my memory of the dark drab space. Later, after I connected with Laëtitia on Instagram, I scrolled through her collection of images. I stopped when I came to one of a single Mallet-Stevens chair on a frosted white background, with sunlight casting interesting shadows on the floor. At first I thought, "A Mallet-Stevens chair. We have several of those!" Then as I looked closer, I recognized the red and amber-colored glass squares next to the stacked corner glass windows of the tower. Laëtitia had taken the photograph during her visit, capturing the interesting composition, surrounded by the dilapidation of the tower.

As they thanked us, we apologized for keeping them so long, "We can be a little verbose, carried away in details," we commented. But they appeared to really enjoy the visit. "I can't believe this house is not better known! It is so incredible!" Jo-ey responded. Laëtitia explained she was still working out her plans for Beeler Gallery, and she asked me to send some additional information that we had discussed during the visit.

I received a kind email from Jo-ey thanking us for our time, telling us how much they enjoyed the tour, and wondering if we would consider allowing them to use our home for some kind of tour as part of Laëtitia's piece for Beeler Gallery. "Of course we would! What an exciting and unexpected reward for all our hard work!" I exclaimed, reading the request to Joe!

Over the next few months, I forwarded an array of photographs, historic letters, and newspaper clippings to Laëtitia as she developed the concept of her artwork that would use Glenbrow as a setting. Although they initially suggested a February date for the event, I worried about the unpredictability of the weather and limitations that winter would hold for prohibiting any outdoor activity. "Snow is lovely, but ice can be an issue, especially with the multiple steps along the walkway," I reminded them. We suggested that they select a date when both indoors and outdoors could be enjoyed. I also pointed out that a tour would require a bus transporting people, as our parking situation was limited. Otherwise, we were looking forward to assisting in any way possible. Soon, we agreed to a hold the event in October. In anticipation of this date, we decided to postpone getting a second dog, a companion to Lola Bola, until after the October art tour. I had promised the kids that we would adopt a puppy this time, which meant a lot of attention, extra cleanup, and work that I knew would fall in my lap.

CHAPTER 19:
Our Summer of Discontent

While awaiting the arrival of spring and the opportunity to get our gardens in order, we planned a trip to Europe—our first real vacation since purchasing the property! The trip was a college graduation present to Maren, and by chance, it coincided with a gathering of Joe's architecture classmates at a celebration of the fiftieth anniversary of Notre Dame's Rome Program. Maren's first visit to Rome would include tours normally not available to the public! We scheduled our trip to allow two weeks' preparation for the spring tour that we were hosting for Columbus Landmarks the first week in May.

The next big project was going to be a new dining room table. Maren and I had advocated for rebuilding the original built-in seating that had been in the "lounge," as it was called on the original blueprints, using it for banquette seating, but Joe wanted to keep the removable wall access so that large pieces of furniture or appliances could be brought in and out of the house. "We also already have the set of eight chairs and recreating new, built-in seating as well as a table is a lot of work!" he reminded us. "Plus, banquette seating is difficult to get in and out of when you have a number of guests." Maren was disappointed. "Someday, when the house is mine, I going to rebuild the built-in sofa that was originally there," she confided.

My initial suggestion for the table centered on a piece that could be broken into parts like the one we had admired during tours of Frank Lloyd

Wright's Kentuck Knob in Pennsylvania. That walnut table featured a thirty-degree angle at the end and seams in the middle of the table, allowing it to be broken into smaller tables for a more intimate setting. I thought this way, we might be able to utilize the space, originally called the lounge, for other purposes. Joe thought the weight of the ash table pieces would make them difficult to move, would require additional legs, as that the split in the table would possibly being an issue. Idea nixed.

Joe focused instead on designing a single dining room table that could accommodate and complement our eight Eames DCW ash chairs. The iconic mid-century modern chairs were purchased along with a black lounge version Eames LCW, several years before *Time* Magazine declared the design the "Chair of the Century." The history of the chair, coupled with its extreme comfort, made it the ideal chair to design a table around for Glenbrow.

In 1940, the Museum of Modern Art in New York held an organic design competition for low-cost furniture and household items for the public. Two young instructors from Cranbrook Art Academy in Bloomfield Hills, Michigan, Charles Eames and Eero Saarinen, entered and won two first prizes in the competition considered by some as the formal beginning of American mid-century modernism. The United States' entry in World War II interrupted production of their collaborative design, and the two parted ways. In 1941, Charles married a Cranbrook art student, Ray Kaiser, who had worked on the competition boards for the MoMa competition. During the war, the husband-and-wife team of Charles and Ray Eames had developed a machine for bending plywood in two directions to make splints for the wounded in World War II, since metal was being used for weaponry. After the war, they used their technique to create comfortable and elegant chairs from bent plywood, placed in production by Hermann Miller in 1946.

Since we had purchased the chairs, ash trees throughout the country had been decimated by the emerald ash borer, creating a limited supply of available wood, which caused Joe to make regular stops at a nearby hardwood lumber supplier in hopes of finding pieces that met his standards. Using our chairs' dimensions, coordinated with ergonomic standards and the size of the dining room, he decided on a nine-foot-long table, forty-two inches wide and slighter lower than average height at twenty-eight inches to acknowledge the slightly lower than average height of the Eames chairs.

Trying to be as environmentally friendly as possible, he purchased a used biscuit joiner on eBay, a tool used to create slots in the edges of wood boards so that an oblong wooden disc, appropriately called a biscuit, can be inserted and glued to fully bond two pieces of wood together. The joiner, a track saw, and both belt and orbital sanders were essential for fabricating the ash boards into a table. The other tool that was essential was a large clamp— very many of them! Soon the studio was cleaned out so that the process of building the table could be started, shielded from the elements.

After returning from Europe, we intended to get right to work, getting the property ready for another Columbus Landmarks Tour, "Glenbrow in Springtime," which was two weeks away in early May. Instead, our focus turned to our eight-year-old lab/border collie rescue, Lola Bola. She had passed her yearly physical two weeks before we left for Europe to update her shots for her stay at Catch-n-Fetch, a nearby facility that offered doggy daycare during the day and boarding overnight. They had sent us photos of her playing and hanging with the other dogs, looking like she was enjoying her stay at camp, even looking like she shed a little winter weight from all the activity. I had Joe film her reaction, expecting her to go ballistic when she saw we had returned, but instead, I received a lukewarm greeting followed by a rush to look out the glass door with her focus on the outdoors.

Once home, the first thing after Lola exited the car was a bout of diarrhea. Thinking she might have picked up a bug during her stay, I called to see if any other dogs had been sick. They had not, and the proprietors said she had seemed fine during her stay. Inside, she had no appetite and began throwing up large amounts of bile, including all over our off-white wool carpet. A trip to the vet checked her for parasites and sent me home with meds for diarrhea and an appetite stimulant. She seemed to be doing better. She started eating, going on walks, and playing with her best friend, Ollie, the blonde lab. Hoping her illness would finally subside, we worked on cleaning up the yard on nice days and steam cleaning the inside on those that were rainy.

During our absence, some varmints decided to make my life more difficult with their nightly forages, tearing up my sedum while looking for grubs. Every morning, I would need to replace the unearthed pieces on the tennis court surface. One of our neighbors adjacent to the tennis court had raccoons in their attic. It wasn't until they were all captured that my sedum was left in peace. Sedum is hardy, though, and after a few rains, it was as good as new.

The Columbus Landmarks tour was scheduled for the first week in May to showcase the house in all its verdant glory, with rhododendrons and azaleas sporting their magenta and deep orange blossoms, the sedum a sea of chartreuse, and various perennials and wildflowers all showing off their vibrant colors. The clay pots around the property had been filled with variegated coleus, geraniums, mixes of edible herbs, and brightly colored creeping Jenny dangling over their rims. Tomatoes and a variety of peppers had been planted and staked in the garden boxes, along with a mixture of rosemary, parsley, and cilantro in between. Unseasonably warm weather in April, along with the spring rains, had caused the leaves to pop, creating a green backdrop behind the house and along the hillside of the ravine. We couldn't wait to show off our landscaping outside and Joe's new furniture on the inside. Unfortunately, the clouds burst open just as the tour began, with the downpour lasting all day. We were able to show off the verdant landscape, but from under umbrellas or through the windows.

After another course of meds, with little appetite and a continual loss of weight, I took Lola Bola back to the vet for a third time, thinking she might have eaten something that was causing a blockage. "She has a history of eating my husband's pajamas if he leaves them on the bed!" I told them. The vet took an X-ray and returned with the worst news possible. Lola had metastatic lung cancer and cardiomegaly. There was nothing they could do, and they suggested we take her home and spoil her for her final days.

The news hit us like a brick wall. Anyone who has ever lost a beloved pet understands the anguish we felt. We had just lost our sixteen-year-old Whisper less than a year before, which was hard enough, but she had lived a long, loving life. Lola had been a loving companion through Maren and Fia's turbulent teenage years. Now we were losing the last connection our children had with their youth, and my constant companion of the last seven-and-a-half years.

Sadness is all-encompassing. The world around me became drab, without color, like waking up in the early hours when objects appear only in sepia tones. Our hearts were so heavy with sadness that everyone retreated into their rooms, taking turns with our beloved Bola. "This can't be right. Bola is only eight years old. She was just playing with Ollie two days ago. Can't we get a second opinion?" asked Fia, inconsolable with tears streaming down her cheeks. "The doctors showed me her X-rays. Her lungs were full of cancer," I informed her. "Let's create a bucket list and make her final days special while we say goodbye."

The next two weeks, the grass didn't get mowed, weeding was put on hold, and chores went undone as our focus went to ensuring Lola Bola's final days were special. We made a Thanksgiving dinner in July. She made trips down to the creek several times a day, with the kids helping her when she became weak. She visited her friend Ollie, a two-year-old lab who seemed to sense her illness and played accordingly. We took Lola to play in the fountains at Capital University, a favorite haunt of hers when we lived in the temporary house while restoring Glenbrow. Lola got her own bowl of ice cream at Graeter's and was able to run free at Wolfe Park on the edge of Alum Creek in Bexley. Pizza, steak, and even fish were on her menu, as every meal was a special treat. We had an early birthday party for her with cake and ice cream.

All the special treatment seemed to perk her up a little, but by the beginning of July, we knew the end was close. The Fourth of July was her least favorite day of the year since she, like many dogs, was terrified of fireworks. She had gone from seventy-four pounds in early April to thirty-two in July, despite her special high carb, fat, and protein diet. By July 2, she needed assistance to go out. I googled what do if your pet died on a holiday, and it said to place the deceased animal in a freezer or make sure you bury them six feet underground. It warned that a shallower grave was likely to get dug up by animals and it was a most unpleasant experience. I was horrified. We all said our goodbyes to our dear family member and made the difficult trip to the animal hospital.

The end to her suffering wasn't the end to ours. The kids didn't go out but instead came home from work and went into their rooms crying. It was so difficult for all of us, but as a stay-at-home mom, I was with her all day, every day. I hated coming home to an empty house without her presence. I started looking for puppies online. We had always adopted rescue dogs, but all the local dogs were pit bulls—a breed that frightens me in that many have been bred to fight, and one that our homeowner's insurance refused to cover. New to the process was the need to fill out applications and get preapproval before adoption. I filled out applications on several rescue sites and while awaiting approval, searched for a pup that could help bring my family out of their depression. "I know a pup won't replace Bola, but she would want another pup to have our family," I explained to the kids.

Hoping to adopt a lab pup, I kept extending the distance until I located a litter of goldadors (golden retriever/Labrador mix) located 108 miles away. The eight-week-old puppies were known as the musical litter—with Do, Re, Mi, Fa, Sol, La, and Ti—and ran the gamut from looking entirely like a golden to being solid black like a lab. By the time I was approved, there were two female pups left, solid-colored La and a black pup with a white front paw named Fa. Since adoption was first come, first served, we got up early on a Sunday morning, driving down to suburban Cincinnati so that we could be the first in line when the adoption site opened. It was Fa that stole our hearts, and soon the adoption was finalized. The rescue had told us they had just spayed and dewormed her, causing her to have a bit of diarrhea. "No worries, we'll take great care for her!" we said, and soon we were driving back to her forever home. Having just returned from Barcelona where we enjoyed the architecture of Gaudí, we decided to name her Milà, in honor of both the famous Gaudí house as well as her musical litter beginnings.

It had been many years since we had had a puppy. In the past, I would go to the shelter in anticipation of adopting a youngster, but often returned with one that had been a problem dog and there the longest. Milà was a true nine-week-old, eight-pound pup, so small you could scoop her up with one hand when she got into her puppy mischief. Born on May 4 ("May the fourth be with you," as the kids joked), she wasn't housebroken and needed constant supervision, as soon became apparent. Joe would say, "Trouble was her middle name." Her black fur was longer and softer than any previous dog we had adopted, with floppy ears that had whisps of wild fur extending from behind. She was playful and full of energy, clumsily slipping as she chased her toys, and I realized it was going to be very difficult to prepare the house for an event.

We found the perfect fit for the dog crate on the ledge between the stone wall and tiled tub enclosure in our bedroom. She was so teeny that we divided the crate into thirds, making it a smaller confined space. We placed towels over her dog bed in case of accidents. She cried when we first placed her into bed for the night, but after reminding her we were only a few feet away, she quickly fell asleep. "Ah . . . I was afraid there were going to be many sleepless nights in our future," I said to Joe as her yelping stopped.

The next morning, I made a Wednesday appointment for her next round of shots and to have her checked out. The animal hospital was so glad to hear we adopted a new pup after seeing how despondent we were over the unexpected and recent loss of our dear Lola Bola. My friend Sarah came over with puppy gifts and to play with Milà. "Oh my god, she's a little ball of fur. So adorable! I want her!" Sarah exclaimed. It was so nice to have joy return to the house.

Early Wednesday morning, I woke to the sound of Milà throwing up. There were puddles of yellow bile soaking into the towel covering her bed.

I removed her, asking Joe to watch her while I cleaned it up. "Shoot!" I heard him cry out "She has diarrhea too!" I heard him say. "Poor pup. Take her outside and watch her closely," I told him, grabbing some paper towels and bleach spray. I cleaned up the bile, then turned to clean the diarrhea, realizing there was a small amount of blood and what looked like a long piece of linguine mixed in with the yellowish stool. Knowing she had only had puppy chow and dog cookies, I decided to place it in a baggie to take to the vet. Joe returned with the pup, who appeared listless. We laid her on the towel-covered bed and she soon began to have a petit mal seizure. Knowing how to handle the situation after living through Whisper's seizure disorder, I remained calm and kept a close eye on her, glad it wasn't as severe as the seizures Whisper would experience. It was only 8:20 in the morning, but I kept calling the vet until someone answered.

I wrapped her in a clean towel, and by shortly after 9:00 a.m., we were at the vet and taken into the room. This once "ball of energy" was listless. I explained how we had only adopted her on Sunday and how I had made an appointment for later today for an initial check-up and her next round of puppy shots. "She had diarrhea just before we adopted her, but she has been fine, and very playful after bringing her home," I told them. Milà had a fever. They drew some blood and took the stool specimen. In a couple of minutes, the doctor returned with a forlorn look and terrible news. Milà had both parvovirus and hookworms, both very serious conditions. "I have heard of parvovirus but really don't know much about it," I explained. "It is very serious and up to 90 percent of dogs with it do not survive. She will need immediate hospitalization. The cost is expensive, and even with great care, many dogs don't survive. On top of the parvo, hookworms are very difficult to treat and very contagious to both other animals and humans who come in contact with the feces," he told us. "I'll have one of our tech's prepare an estimate for you to decide whether to treat her." I replied, "She's our pup. We just lost our Lola and can't even bear to think of losing her. Of course we'll treat her." Unbearable! My heart swelled with grief! Again! "How will we tell the kids?" I asked Joe, as the tears poured from both of us. We kissed our sweet pup goodbye as the doctor promised to give us regular updates. "Feel free to call at any time," Dr. Connell told me. "I know how you just lost Lola and this must be so hard on you guys." We returned home to the empty house, dreading having to tell Maren and Fia. On top of the grief was the need to disinfect our house and yard from the hookworm contamination.

It was a trying week. Milà was hospitalized until the end of office hours on Saturday, and then it was up to us to carry her through the critical next seventy-two hours. She seemed better when we picked her up on Saturday afternoon. Dr. Connell came out to tell me, "She seems to be responding well to the treatment, but the most important thing is to keep her hydrated. She is perky right now because she just finished an IV. Here is my cell phone. I will check in on her, but please don't hesitate to call if you have any questions." She went over several meds that Milà needed, while also setting up an appointment for Monday morning.

By the time we returned home, Milà had become languid, with her eyes dull and lacking the sparkle of her previous self. She had been sent home with several medicines, including one that had to be administered through a small syringe. She was so lethargic that she refused water. I washed the used syringe with hot soapy water and used it to shoot water down the back of her throat. Turning to an online Facebook group for older dogs that I belonged to, I received the advice of trying an unflavored form of Pedialyte, a liquid used for dehydration in babies. Based on a suggestion by the vet, I gave her three ccs of the clear liquid every fifteen minutes to keep her hydrated. It was a long weekend with little sleep, but by Monday, I saw marked improvement! She returned to eating, no doubt aided by my addition of chicken breast and cut-up veggies to her food. Soon she was the holy terror one would expect from a puppy!

CHAPTER 20:
Back to Work

With the pup feeling better, our efforts turned to preparing the property, neglected in recent weeks while we cared for our ailing dogs. "It doesn't take long for weeds to take over," I told Joe as I was bent over with my blue-stemmed dandelion tool, extracting the long roots of various plants. Joe had set up two large wire compost bins behind the pine trees, just beyond the tennis court. "Try to layer the bins in both green and brown plant material," he would remind me. Despite each bin being a four-foot square, they would quickly fill up and when he wasn't looking, I would sneak over to the edge of the ravine and deposit piles down the slope as well. I figured the growing piles of ornamental grasses and branches I deposited would make nice nests for animals once cold weather set in.

We received a request to present a short program on our restoration to the staff of the Frank Lloyd Wright Westcott House in Springfield, Ohio. The presentation was to be followed by a site visit for the staff on a later date to tour Glenbrow in the morning and Ted van Fossen's Rush Creek Village in Worthington in the afternoon. We used the slideshow we had prepared for the Columbus Landmarks talk and knew the material like the back of our hands, so minus the time for the short trip back and forth, it would not require much of our time. We were to meet at the Westcott Solar House, a learning space located just north of the carriage house on the property. The audience included staff members and docents, all well-versed on the history of Wright at the time of his prairie houses in the early twentieth century. The purpose of the talk and tour was to present Wright's later Usonian design principles that were adopted at Glenbrow and their later evolution that had been realized by van Fossen. This would convey the influence of Wright's organic design principles on the built environment.

A couple weeks after the talk, a group of Westcott docents visited Glenbrow on a warm sunny morning and then we joined them after lunch for a tour of several of Ted van Fossen's Rush Creek Village (RCV) homes in Worthington. Although Joe and I had toured several RCV houses in the past, it would be Maren's first time, as well as our first time visiting the recently renovated Martha Wakefield house—the original home that started the whole fifty-home community. The house had been sold in poor shape that had required much restoration work, but there were still some incredible original details, including a perforated sliding panel in wood at the front window, as well as a geometric appliqué on and above one of the doors.

By the middle of August, Joe had completed work on the ash dining room table. The tabletop, along with its two support elements, were being coated with polyurethane in the studio. "The four of us can carry the tabletop from the studio into the house in one load and then later bring the bases. Then I'll assemble it the dining room," Joe suggested. This concept was soon discarded when he asked me and the kids to help him flip over the top to coat the opposite side with polyurethane. "You have to be kidding!" I said, as Fia and I struggled to even lift the three-and-a-half-foot-by-nine-foot ash top to flip it. "There is no way that we are going to be able to carry it, let alone down several steps. After all the work you did, do you really want to risk ruining it?" I asked. "We're not strong enough! Call the movers that we used to carry the range into the kitchen."

Joe scheduled Adam to work with him on the tower the day the movers were scheduled. Just prior to their arrival, he and Joe opened the removable wall panel in the dining room that formed the back to the storage closet just outside the kitchen door, as we had intended for bringing in large items. The tight turns in the entranceway, along with the low ceilings, had convinced

Joe to create another more manageable access point. Although the French doors along the ravine were wide enough, the difficulty in getting to them had led Joe to design the concealed wall panel, creating a four-foot-by-six-foot temporary opening.

The final piece of large permanent furniture was situated in the dining room, replacing the temporary six-foot butcher block top with the steel hairpin legs. Visually, the scale of the table seemed large at first, but the eight DCW plywood Eames chairs fit perfectly, and within a few days, the piece seemed to be the perfect size for the room. It was designed as both an homage to the furniture designs of Schindler as well as incorporating elements of Wright's Usonian tables. Both design aspects were in harmony with the original details of the house. Historic photographs of Glenbrow included a small round table, designed for the house by Ted van Fossen and fabricated at a later date. As with almost all of the original furniture, it had been stolen or damaged beyond repair before our purchase of the house. The round table was present when the house first went on the market in 2006, but it had disappeared one day while the realtor was showing the house. The new ash table allowed Joe to add another permanent design element that worked perfectly for our family's entertaining needs. Now that the table was in place, we were ready for entertaining!

With much of the summer focused on caring for pets, the landscape required some attention at the same time the dog days of summer set in. The chore I dread the most, and a job I had perfected over time—pulling poison ivy—required me to wear a Tyvek suit and don shoulder-length, chemical-resistant gloves. This protective gear may be great for preventing a reaction to poison ivy, but the materials simply do not breathe. I needed a day with early morning temperatures below seventy degrees, with the ground wet enough to assist me in extracting the fibrous roots. I've learned over time to scout out areas with the ivy before I gown up, to enable me to act quickly while wearing my uncomfortable gear.

After a heavy downpour the night before, I rose just after dawn and dressed for my work: long-sleeve linen on top, with linen pants, knee socks, and rain boots below. I carefully climbed into the white Tyvek jumpsuit, mindful as I pulled the attached foot covers over the boots so as not to damage the fabric of the suit. I wore a brimmed sun hat with a chin strap for tightness, then pulled the jumpsuit hood over my hat, and zipped the front to just below my chin. Over the hood I place a respirator mask, which secured my glasses while protecting my face from possible droplets of urushiol that can be released as I pull a vine from the ground. Lastly on top, I donned a pair of disposable nitrile gloves, pulling up the shoulder-length, chemical-resistant gloves for the final layer of protection. I looked as if I was ready for a lunar walk as I prepared two heavy-duty contractor bags, taking one with me while leaving the second for backup preparation.

There is something almost zen-like in weeding. Your mind focuses on the chore at hand with only an occasional distraction from nature. All the problems of daily life fade, leaving your mind focused on the task at hand. Your concentration must be even sharper when pulling poison ivy. Any haphazard mistake might cause weeks of suffering due to the urushiol toxin. The eyes scan the brush in search of the three-leaf menace, gingerly lifting the surrounding branches to expose the root. Occasionally, lifting a branch can startle you, especially in late summer when the black water snakes are feeding in preparation for their long winter hibernation, digesting the unfortunate rodent that had become a last meal. Best to move on and allow the snake to digest in peace.

After extracting the fibrous root, you must carefully entwine it so it does not touch any part of your exposed face, then discard it into the bag. Since your gloves are contaminated, any itch of your nose, droop of your glasses, or tilt of your hat must be ignored. If Joe is around, I will usually ask him for an adjustment. An occasional low branch may cause a jolt to the head. An unexpected rut can trip you. The most difficult terrain on the property is by far the ravine, with its often-hidden animal holes. Wet from the morning dew, it was also slippery in the built-in shoe covers of the suit.

As the morning proceeded, the temperature rose to an uncomfortable level. The suit doesn't breathe, not even a little. I often wondered how those fighting a life-threatening disease in sub-Saharan Africa can function, as rivers of sweat ran down my arms to form small puddles in the fingertips of the inner gloves. When the heat becomes unbearable, it's time to quit. The full bag of the nasty ivy was tied and then discarded into the already opened trash container. Next came the shoulder-length gloves, carefully pulled from the tips of the fingers and removed without touching other parts of the suit, then also dropped into the can. The inner pair of gloves, having been protected, are used to remove the hat, unzip the front of the suit (still careful not to touch your chin), and then to slide the suit off the shoulders. A rush of cool air provides a welcome sense of relief as you realize your clothes are sticking to your body, dripping with sweat. Careful to touch only the inside layer, I pulled off the suit, also discarding it in the trash container. Finally, the inner nitrile gloves were removed, their tips weighed down from the collection of sweat. Off to the shower, cold water at first to keep pores closed, then, after the first wash, normal water temperature can resume. Crazy? Maybe! But this technique has kept me free of the vile rash and interminable itch. I've been told the native plant known as jewel weed, a tall and hollow stemmed plant with oval shaped leaves and an orange flower, can be mashed and used as a treatment, but as the old adage goes, an ounce of prevention is worth a pound of cure.

CHAPTER 21:
Concept to Construct

During the summer, the communication necessary to finalize Beeler Gallery's use of Glenbrow began to transpire on a frequent basis. We discovered that Laëtitia's work was to be sponsored by Expo Chicago, an international exposition of contemporary and modern art, *Art in America*, and the Cultural Services of the French Embassy in the United States. With Laëtitia in Paris finalizing her concept, Jo-ey requested additional information for her and brought individuals involved with Beeler's upcoming season through the house for tours to enable them to get a sense of the space prior to the event. *Season Two* was Jo-ey Tang's second year as Director of Exhibitions at Beeler Gallery. The second season, entitled *Follow the Mud*, was to be a series of Instances, of which our house was going to be used for the second of eight total. *EXPOSURE* was to be "a performative and interpretive tour using the site to explore the unconscious undercurrents of design in the human condition." Jo-ey engaged Danny Marcus, an art historian and the Roy Lichtenstein Fellow at the Columbus Museum of Art, to write the text for *EXPOSURE* that would be included in the announcement as well as on a poster for the event being created by Vier5, a Paris-based visual communication firm known for their cutting-edge designs. Danny had toured the house over the summer and later interviewed me, requesting documents to aid in his writing.

Beeler held an open call for performers and dancers, providing us with additional clues that Laëtitia's piece was going to be more performance-orientated rather than an installation. An announcement for attending the event went out in a press release by Beeler Gallery with an RSVP due to limited capacity, which was almost immediately filled with a waiting list.

It was difficult getting a house ready for a performance with a wild pup around. Milà was turning five months old the week before the performance, thankfully just old enough to be vaccinated and accepted into an obedience training program. "Her middle name is trouble," I would repeat to myself, as every job would need to be repeated as she left a trail of havoc wherever she roamed. We scheduled her to enter a two-week program, allowing us to have five days to put the finishing touches on the property. You never realize how much time a puppy requires until you need to accomplish work by a set date. As much as we missed her, her departure to Canine College made our tasks immensely easier.

CHAPTER 22:
Towering Task Ahead

We had decided that the purpose of the tower was to be short-term rental, perhaps an artist's retreat that would inspire creativity in the biophilic setting. Several steps down from the driveway elevation, the ground floor would house a library and a large worktable facing the creek, where guests could spread out their work while they enjoyed the view. The entrance level would have a small kitchen with an eat-in island and living room. Up a flight of stairs, the third level would feature a bedroom with a vista, high in the canopy of the trees, as well as an en suite bathroom. The top floor would be the roof terrace with outdoor seating. The tower would produce income during our retirement and allow us to meet interesting people who would be attracted to the unique setting and organic design. We could choose when we wanted guests and close during the winter months so that we could travel. We would offer a curated wine and spirits list for those who stayed and thought other offerings might be added as we saw fit. Grand plans, but first we had a lot of work to do.

Joe and Adam had been working on the tower over the summer and into the fall. The top roof above the winding stairwell had been replaced in November of 2018, but other major sources of water leaks were due to design flaws on the roof terrace. Joe had previously placed some temporary felt-paper patches until a real solution—removal, fabricating sloping triangular crickets on top of the roof's deck to ensure proper drainage, and replacement of the roof membrane—could be undertaken.

Inside, many years of leaks had left some of the framing and subfloor in very poor condition, especially on the eastern edge of the building, which had rotting parts of an entire corner area from the topmost roof terrace all the way down to the ground floor. Doors and walls had delaminated, parquet floors were badly buckled, and there was so much mold that we had hired a mold remediation company after we first acquired the property. The interior was so dilapidated that drywall was removed from the studs and wood paneling was discarded. The remaining built-in furniture was in too poor a condition to restore. Broken windows and openings to the outdoors had been closed with plastic sheeting in order to temporarily seal the building until a time when we were ready to work its restoration. Although it was built in the mid-1960s, the roof leaks had left the condition of building worse than the 1940s main house.

While removing the old roof material from the terrace, they discovered a large beehive within a rotten section of parapet wall. We called in a friend who had taken up beekeeping as a hobby to come in and remove the hive. Steve, a commercial airline pilot by profession, arrived the next day with full gear. He donned a Tyvek suit, a white, large-brimmed hat with netting draping down over his shoulders, gloves, and boots, and he carried a bee smoker. "We're gonna smoke 'em out!" he explained, in his bad George W. Bush impersonation, as he turned to climb up the stairs, a trail of smoke following his ascent.

To correct the design flaw of the terrace, Joe and Adam built crickets to keep rainwater from collecting at corners and edges, directing it to flow to the new scupper spout and off the roof and down to the creek. Joe designed the new scupper to also act as a water feature, extending out from the terrace-side railing to allow the draining water to be visible from the floors below. The new strand board surfaces of the crickets were edged with cedar-beveled siding to taper them to the existing plywood deck, with a layer of half-inch rigid insulation and finally, the reinforced EPDM rubber roof membrane. Eventually, we will install a floating teak roof deck system on adjustable feet to create a level surface with the water draining below the deck. The creek edge of the terrace will feature a long, built-in bench with a hinged top that will allow access to clean the scupper drain.

They also repaired and rebuilt the original trellis that extended off the stairway roof and over the terrace that was in poor shape. Instead of removing the original beams, they applied a top piece of rubber to them and then sistered new one-by-twelve cedar boards on each side to cover them, which also makes them more visually prominent and in scale with the entire building. Originally, three fins extended vertically from the trellis and engaged the side of the terrace wall on the stuccoed surface of the northwest side of the building. The location of these vertical fins determined the edge of the projecting bay created for the new egress window for the bedroom level.

On the exterior wood portion that faced the creek, they also rebuilt parts of the compromised structure and fabricated a *brise-soleil* to reinstate the former twelve-inch spacing of the original fixed window glass wall facing the creek. This would also serve as a scaffolding to install the new operable windows on the ravine side's steep slope. The eight-by-ten-foot element was fabricated on the ground out of cedar two-by-fours, stained and then hoisted in place by way of a winch. Joe thought that in concept, it would not be too difficult to hoist it into position. The reality was that much muscle and a lot of prayers were required to even get it down the hill, let alone lift up the structure to the third floor to rest on the cedar gerberettes extruding from the paired floor beams—a solution borrowed from Centre Pompidou in Paris. The third-floor bedroom would have aluminum-clad-wood, three-by-six-foot operable windows, which needed to be installed from the exterior. The *brise-soleil* has a deck of cedar struts on top of the projecting gerberettes that accommodated the difficult window installation, as well as a means to clean and maintain the window wall in the future.

To bring the third-floor bedroom up to code, an egress window facing the pond was added that would allow a safe escape to the carport roof, since the creek-side windows were high above the steeply sloping ground. Original tower plans included a door where we were adding the egress window, although it was never built. The new window opening required sawing through the stucco wall, the remnants of which were extremely heavy. The window placement was determined by the aforementioned three fins that extended down the wall from the rooftop trellis. After the egress window was positioned, it left a narrow vertical opening that Joe would divide into four square segments. We thought of adding squares of stained glass that matched others on the building, but instead we used a piece of thick translucent resin with an embedded layer of seagrass. For both aesthetic and privacy reasons, we also used this material in the adjoining bathroom to replace a floor-to-ceiling window directly opposite the toilet that overlooked the rear deck of the neighbor's house. The random vertical pattern of the grass was apparent from the inside but appeared as a solid frosted glass when viewed from the exterior. The room was much brighter with the green seagrass enhancing the biophilic environment we sought to create.

The windows overlooking the ravine at the entrance level were originally, like those on the second floor, much smaller and inoperable. Positioned above Mr. Gunning's credenza, they were about four feet tall, at the level of the credenza that was removed. Two extension ladders were positioned into the sloping ground of the ravine to install the new windows.

There were also two entry doors on this level that were adjacent to each other in a corner that hit each other when they both were open. We removed one to simplify the entry vestibule so that the interior would function more efficiently as a living room and kitchenette. The original doors had literally disintegrated over the years of neglect. We decided to replace them with a steel-insulated door with horizontal slot windows, which added light to the dark space. This was also done at the top of the stairs going out to the roof terrace, which also brought daylight to a windowless space. We also decided to make use of five pieces of insulating glass that had been mismeasured years earlier for the kitchen in the main house, using them for a strip of windows in the kitchenette, living room, and around a corner in the entry where the removed door had been. This brought in daylight form all four sides of the space.

Prior to the mid-1960s tower, there had been a single-story block building that housed a kiln the Gunnings used for art projects. Without the original plans of the structure that housed the kiln, Joe surmised that the new floor joists were added above the roof rafters of the one-story building when it was vertically extended to become the tower. He and Adam removed these nonfunctioning lower joists, which gave them the room to build a new floor with a vapor barrier on top of the old concrete floor, providing an insulated floor that matched those on the upper levels, instead of a cold and very unlevel concrete floor. The original parquet floor, removed due to stains and warping, would be replaced with a new oak parquet floor. The new windows facing the creek would be positioned in a new bay that cantilevered slightly past the foundation wall, giving us a bit more room at this level.

Although buried into the sloping terrain, there were still issues to contend with while installing the windows and replacing the wood trim that surrounded them. On the creek side would be three operable, three-by-six-foot casement windows, like those used in the third-level bedroom floor, as well as in our bedroom suite in the main house. The original block kiln structure's walls were out of square, so the northeast corner was cocked in plan by approximately five inches, making the existing footprint a slight trapezoid. When the structure was converted to the tower in the mid 1960s, they built the new walls above so the tower's footprint was in square. They extended their new studs down and in front of the old concrete block wall and covered everything in stucco. Now, the interior of this crooked concrete block wall would be treated similarly with new studs inside (needed for insulation as well) to straighten it out.

With the structure all corrected, and with the new windows and new roof complete, the interior living spaces were now the focus. The work would progress from the top down—from the roof terrace down to the ground. New interior framing along the perimeter walls would provide ample space for insulation as well as leaving a thermal gap between the old stud wall and this new one. After the new layout was decided, walls were built on each floor to separate the bathroom, enclose the kitchen cabinetry, and conceal mechanicals. New subfloor was laid to replace the rotted compromised pieces.

The third floor, just below the roof terrace, would serve as a bedroom and bathroom with natural light on all four sides of the room. The new wall that separated the bedroom from the bathroom followed the angled line of the stairs and allowed both privacy for the bathroom and built-in features for the bed. Sunlight filtered through the foliage of the tree canopy to create shadows that slowly moved across the floor as the sun traversed the sky. Remnants of vine, which had enveloped the entire tower when we first discovered it on that warm September afternoon, still clung to the vertical panes of plate glass on the southwest corner of the third floor. The layout of the bathroom would optimize access to plumbing and ductwork for the HVAC system, while translucent seagrass windows and stained glass provided both light and privacy. Tucked into the corner of the stairway would be a stackable washer and dryer.

The main entrance level on the second floor contains both a living room and kitchenette. Below the windows along the creek, Joe and Adam built the framework for a built-in sofa with tables at each end, using wood recycled from the framing around the old windows. The kitchenette layout would feature a peninsula for preparation and dining that extended to form the countertop and two small work areas: one for a sink and dishwasher, the other for a small cooktop, oven, and refrigerator. Across from the peninsula (that I erroneously call an island), would remain the original coat closet.

The ground level was to host a library for Joe's collection of art and architecture books as well as the six-foot butcher block table with steel hairpin legs that had served as our temporary dining table before the ash table Joe fabricated was completed. Guests would have a large workspace with an incredible view of the ravine. With the floor raised for insulation, the room would be much warmer than the original concrete floor slab. Eventually, new oak parquet floor, consistent with the other floors, would be added. The room would also house a small utility room with the old door on this level as an emergency egress that could also serve as a potential separate entrance to the library.

There were concrete stucco remnants from work on the tower, so instead of sending them off to become landfill, we put them to good use. Behind the main house, we decided to add another gabion wall, this one only two feet tall, parallel with the ravine-side planter outside of the dining room, leaving enough space between them for a walkway. "Maren and I can do all the work after the cages are constructed," I told Joe. The purpose of the wall was to prevent erosion so we could create a flat stone path that would not be washed away by the rain. There would be a total of five sections, each four feet in length for a total of twenty feet. Ultimately, we hope to extend a path all the way down to the creek.

Instead of using aggregate only a few inches long, we planned on using rounded creek rock that Maren and I had been collecting during our trips down to the stream with the pup. Joe assembled the cages, each buried a few inches into the ground, then secured in them place with stakes to prevent movement. After filling the belowground portion built into the side of the hill with rubble from around the tower, I started filling the cages with creek stone. We thought we had amassed quite a bit until I started filling the bins and quickly ran out. With just weeks before the event, I talked Joe into going to a stone yard I had visited in the past, where we could more easily find the rocks I needed without making difficult trips up the steep hillside. Plastic was laid in the rear of the car before visiting a nearby yard where I had previously found a good assortment of sizes and types of stone. We decided on a Canadian river stone, each about the size of a grapefruit. After filling the car with what we thought to be enough, we returned for another load, and another. Despite their larger size, it was apparent that completion before the event was impossible, as there was still so much to do. "Attendees will have to view a work in progress," I told Joe.

Knowing the art event was upcoming, Joe worked on the tower restoration up until about a week before the event date, leaving time to clean up the demolition debris he had accumulated and removed during the previous months. Any salvable wood was piled into the carport for possible future use on accent walls, while a dumpster was brought in for the rest. After raking up the area around the tower during the cleanup, Maren noticed the top of a smooth rock between the tower and the last bay of the carport. She started to dig around the edges as I returned to weed the garden.

After about fifteen minutes, Maren reappeared to show off a basketball-sized object. "Look what I found!" she exclaimed, rolling the object toward me due to its weight. "Wow, that's cool! I wonder if it's an ornamental sphere from some building?" I wondered. The ringed object was almost perfectly round in mottled grays and browns. "I'll post a picture on Facebook and ask Nora and Grace if it looks familiar to them." In our initial weeding around the fern garden after we took ownership of the property, I found a two-foot-square, limestone, pyramid-shaped capstone, an architectural artifact from some building that had been buried under years of leaves, fallen branches, and vines. Perhaps this was another remnant from a building. Regardless, it was more buried treasure!

I posted the photograph of the object on Facebook, tagging Nora and Grace to see if I might discover a little history about it. Before long, someone commented that it was a concretion and that there might well be fossils inside. I had never heard of a concretion before, but after a quick search online, I discovered carbonate concretions are caused by organic material compaction in shale. They can be found in central Ohio and are remnants from the Devonian Age, around 360 million years ago. After reading about them, I realized I had found other examples, some still embedded in the surrounding rock. Although they may not be very valuable, they are an interesting geological find.

CHAPTER 23:
Hint of Things to Come

L aëtitia returned to Columbus in September to prepare for her show at Beeler Gallery. She scheduled a rehearsal with the performers on site, about two weeks before the event, to give them an understanding of the layout of the spaces and to practice their parts. It also provided the support staff a chance to take final measurements for props that would be utilized during the performance and gave us additional clues about what was to come.

I greeted Laëtitia, whom I had not seen since her initial visit on that frigid winter day. "Welcome back! I'm glad the weather is so much more pleasant than last time you were here," I exclaimed, greeting her like an old friend after corresponding with her over the months. Jo-ey introduced about a dozen young performers and support people who would take part in the performance piece. "Welcome everyone!" I presented a brief history of the site for them and led them toward the front door. "Joe and I will stay out of your way. There is iced tea on the counter. Please let me know if there is anything you would like me to do." Spotting the recently discovered concretion, I said, "Look at what Maren discovered when we were cleaning up by the tower yesterday!" "So cool! It's a concretion—I have one at home," Laëtitia commented. "It's over 300 million years old," I replied. "That is so cool!" Jo-ey added, taking photos of our newly found treasure. The group went inside and began their rehearsing right away.

Ian Ruffino, one of the curators at Beeler, came separately with a few more participants. He brought tools along with him and discussed some of the plans with Joe, which included cutting sheets of Masonite for a tap dance platform. He also asked if we would mind if a bar was set up in our bedroom, and whether they could fill the tub with ice to store the cocktail mix. Ian took measurements in our bedroom in preparation for building a bar on the bathtub's elevated plinth. "Laëtitia had a special symbolic cocktail created for the occasion," we were informed.

On my end, I worked on a floor plan with a key to our collection of artwork and custom furniture. Prior to having children, Joe and I collected art created by many of our artist friends; we also purchased pieces for gifts on milestone birthdays and other special occasions. I had never really considered the amount of work we had acquired until the task of packing it up for the move. Now I was made aware that we had accumulated much more than I ever would have thought! Expecting there to be a couple of dozen, I was shocked when the key listed over eighty works—yet another example of the hoarder gene resurfacing! We have a lot of friends who are artists, so supporting their work is understandable, and our previous Noverre Musson house, with ample wall space to display our collection, was the perfect place.

We scheduled a dinner for Laëtitia and Beeler Gallery staff a week out from the event. I knew they were busy preparing the gallery for the opening, but offered, suggesting, "You need a dinner break, and it will allow a final evaluation of the site." I baked bread and harvested the final heirloom tomatoes and peppers still growing in my garden to include in a roasted vegetable sauce, while Joe made fresh pasta. Of course, there was a lot of wine and grappa! It was also a special dinner to christen the table Joe had recently completed, allowing us to now easily seat eight. We were presented a lovely gift—a set of a dozen cocktail glasses with the *EXPOSURE* graphics designed by the cutting-edge French visual communication firm, Vier5! *EXPOSURE* was the name of the second Instance of Laëtitia's *Follow the Mud* series for Beeler Gallery. Thanking them for their thoughtful gift, I commented, "I love these! Now I will have a permanent collection to serve at future dinner parties to bring back the wonderful memories of this experience!" A battery of correspondences arrived in final preparation for the Sunday event, making me thankful we were only responsible for the site.

The house preparation was made infinitely easier when our five-month-old puppy, Milà, left for training camp. I must admit I get like a crazy woman once the house is cleaned for an event. "You wouldn't want anyone to think someone actually lives in this house!" Maren would quip, rolling her eyes as I constantly reminded her to put things away instead of abiding by her usual "where it lays is where it stays" attitude.

Since starting the restoration project nearly five years earlier, our lives had gotten much more casual; linen and cotton casual wear in warm weather and wool and jeans when it's cold. During several rounds of downsizing prior to the final move, I donated most of my good clothes, realizing that I hardly ever wore them and didn't have room with the limited closet space at Glenbrow. Thinking about what I would wear for the gallery opening started to preoccupy my mind in late summer as I started looking at thrift stores for an outfit for this rare special event in our lives. Besides the opening, we were invited to join the curators and artists for a dinner celebrating the opening afterward. How often does an event like this happen in one's life? For us, this was an exciting event!

In late summer heat, one anticipates the cool crisp weather of an October evening, so with dreams of more pleasant temperatures in mind, I purchased a vintage black velvet oversized dress by the artist J. Morgan Puett, whose handmade signature line I used to carry in my store. Puett had abandoned her line of clothing years prior and now focuses on Mildred's Lane, a working-living-researching experiment promoting social engagement at a ninety-four-acre artist community, making her previous handmade clothing items now collectible pieces. I made an offer on one of her dresses on eBay that was accepted. I couldn't wait to wear it.

After a hot, dry September, I was worried about an abrupt change in weather. Cold winds shifting from the north could produce a sudden wind event that could prematurely strip the foliage from the dry trees, diminishing the charm of the landscape. My flower gardens were still in bloom thanks to regular watering, and the leaves were just starting to change color. A week prior the event, I started watching weather forecasts, praying for continued dry weather so that rain wouldn't prevent outdoor activity like we had experienced during the May Landmarks tour. The weather gods overcompensated, keeping the cold weather at bay, but on the Thursday of Beeler Gallery opening, temperatures reached nearly ninety degrees. Too warm to even think about a long-sleeve velvet dress! At the last minute, I decided on a sleeveless, black linen, empire waist, floor-length Flax dress with a three-quarter-length sleeve with a crinkled weave linen wrap on top. A mustard-colored wood bracelet that I purchased at the Picasso Museum in Barcelona added color.

Season Two: Follow the Mud, was organized by Jo-ey Tang and cocurators Ian Ruffino and Marla Roddy, around a series of *"INSTANCES—* installations, performances, screenings and dialogs through which voices, sounds, objects, spaces, images, movements, and text that were used to explore how hidden, suppressed and forgotten histories in art, architecture and politics allow individual subjectivities and personal narratives to re-emerge." There were a total of eight Instances after an initial art bookfair held in New York at MoMA PS1 in September. The curated program then moved to Columbus with the opening of *Season Two: Follow the Mud* on October 10. In addition to Laëtitia, the program included sculptor/filmmaker/ educator Michael Stickrod, as well as his video collaboration with French photographer/auteur filmmaker Michel Auder, and a sound performance by experimental musician/artist C. Spencer Yeh. We had been curiously anticipating what the artists had conceived over the preceding months and looked forward to the opening as well as the entire season.

Beeler Gallery features a 6,000-square-foot exhibition space and a ninety-nine-seat screening room located on the campus of Columbus College of Art and Design, adjacent to the Columbus Museum of Art in Columbus's Discovery District. On previous visits to Beeler Gallery, the cavernous open spaces were silent, with lighting focused on the displayed art, but with the opening, the entrance to the gallery space was bustling with people crowded just outside the galleries. Hanging from the exposed bar joists of the tall ceiling was a twenty-foot-long banner made of strips of burlap and a gridded fabric. The fabric was covered with segments of text announcing the "Instances" in the font I recognized from the Vier5 cocktail glasses that I had recently received as a gift.

Jo-ey presented a brief introduction of the visiting artists, giving some background on the project and welcoming attendees to experience *Instance No. 1: WATER.* We made our way past a recreation of the ticket booth from the Museum of Modern Art in Kamakura, Japan, a site that Badaut Haussmann visited during an artist's residency, and into the large gallery spaces. The usual silent backdrop was filled with activity as docents directed attendees into the spacious galleries.

Laëtitia's work often uses historical references to architecture, cinema, and literature—particularly in her the use of allegory to explore how narrative forms of time and memory can free the mind to new realms of thinking and to better understand our own reality. After admiring the reimagined ticket booth at the entrance, we ventured inside the galleries, where we were met with temporary walls defined by shimmering white iridescent drapes descending from the high ceilings to form notional rooms and boundaries. Overhead lights glistened off the undulating fabric that delineated the floor plan of the iconic modernist Museum of Modern Art—Kamakura, the first Japanese museum for contemporary art. Overlooking a prominent reflecting pond, the museum was designed by Le Corbusier protege Sakakura Junzo, and opened in 1951. The museum closed in 2016, transitioning over the course of several decades from a space exhibiting modern art to one featuring Shinto relics. Badaut Haussmann created a ghost-like homage to the former museum while also evoking the rippling effects of water. Throughout the gallery spaces formed by the reflective fabric, were objects that referenced both time and history. An ethereal pyramid of white silica sand evoked the sands of time from an hourglass. A replica of a bamboo stool (once erroneously attributed to Le Corbusier collaborator Charlotte Perriand) and a winged metal light fixture were both references to architectural relics from the past.

Along the silvery pathway was a room aglow in a faint orange light. Inside, artist Michael Stickrod covered the floor in dried goldenrod, accented by warm lighting. Stickrod collaborated with Michel Auder on several pieces throughout the gallery. Stacked pieces of rough timber beams formed seating around video monitors, showing fragments of Auder's cinematography. Filmed in the Auder's distinctive style of cinema verité in the late sixties and early seventies and recently edited by Stickrod, they featured Warhol superstar (and Auder's former wife), Viva. In the large open space, the skeletal form of overturned metal bleachers provided an enclosure around custom conical speakers that Stickrod fabricated and used to amplify Yeh's experimental violin performance.

Afterward, there was a reception for the artists held in the lobby. Usually, this means Joe and I, both introverts, grab a glass of wine and find a secluded corner as we attempt to melt into the background. Having spent months communicating with many of the people involved in the exhibition, however, we were much more comfortable within this environment. We congratulated Laëtitia on her opening after a warm embrace. "Wow! What a stunning show! We had no idea what to expect. The drapery was so ethereal!" We discussed the Kamakura ticket booth and she told us the bamboo chair's fabrication was based upon the size of her young daughter, Anna. Jo-ey came up and we shared our praise for his efforts. "We'll be meeting at Comune on Parsons Avenue for dinner after the reception. Have you been there?" he asked. We hadn't, but he assured us that we would love the restaurant.

From a distance, I spotted Michael Stickrod, whom I had never met. Michael was tall and burly with a look that might have come out of central casting for a Brooklyn artist. Joe and I introduced ourselves, explaining that Laëtitia was using our house as the site for the next Instance. "Oh, you are Joe and Dorri. I heard your home is beautiful!" Michael replied. "Yeah, we are really excited to see what she has in store there! All we know is our bathroom will host a bar, there will be a special cocktail, and there are tap dancers involved! I really enjoyed your pieces in the show," I commented. "Were the cone-shaped pieces speakers?" I asked Michael. "Yeah, I took an existing speaker and fabricated the piece out of metal," he replied. "It was really cool looking. I heard that you live on a farm in Granville with a great studio space in an old barn? I saw Laëtitia's photos from when she visited last winter." Michael chuckled, "They braved the cold and mud on that day!"

Michael introduced us to Michel Auder, who we had only known from his reputation as a filmmaker as a part of Warhol's inner circle. We knew he had been married to Warhol superstar, Viva, and that she had starred in several of his films. Michel had silvery long hair, was dressed in a black blazer over a black sweater, and was as charming as his French accent. We learned that Michael and Michel had met while Michael was a student of his at Yale and that they had collaborated together on projects for many years. "Joe and Dorri own the Usonian house that Laëtitia is using for her piece on Sunday." "Oh, I am sorry I will miss it. I am flying out to Paris on Saturday," Michel replied. "We would love to give you a tour on Friday, if you are available?" I replied. Michael said he was picking Michel up to take him to Granville for lunch on Friday. "Would it be possible to come by around 10 a.m.?" he asked. "Absolutely! We are right on Broad Street, so it will be on your way to Granville!" I replied.

Jo-ey approached us to tell us he would be closing up the gallery and that we would all meet at Comune for dinner. "We have a room reserved and Ian is heading over there now," he told us.

We turned the corner after parking our car, to see Laëtitia and Michel entering the restaurant. Comune is located on the edge of German Village in an old brick storefront that has been freshly painted white. The minimalist white interior features exposed ductwork running beneath the wood trusses at the ceiling and has a linear wooden bench along the wall with simple wooden tables and chairs. We were guided to a room in the rear of the restaurant with a wall of large sliding doors that were open to a courtyard that took advantage of the unseasonably warm weather. The narrow room had a long dark bench along the wall and a single white shelf above with a line of white pots, each holding a single tall, slender succulent. The table was set with tall, elongated wine glasses and black napkins on a white marble top. Black cords dangled from the ceiling to suspend glass orbs that each nestled a single lightbulb.

Michel and Laëtitia were already seated on the bench with their backs against the wall, so we sat directly across from them. Ian arrived just behind us, accompanied by his girlfriend, Dru, whom he introduced. Laëtitia must have eaten there before, because she suggested a wonderful orange wine before peering at the wine list. As the others arrived, the table filled, and soon their voices filled the warm air. We were introduced to Michael Stickrod's wife, Erin, a doctor of homeopathic medicine who sat next to Michel. Other than Michel, Joe and I were the oldest people by almost twenty years. While shared worldviews may erase any age differences, diminished hearing in loud restaurants does not! We both sometimes struggle to hear conversations in noisy spaces—a condition I have become more aware of in recent years.

The long table filled with guests, and wine was poured. The orange wine recommended by Laëtitia was especially delicious, as were several other bottles that followed. As more and more wine was consumed, the room's volume level increased, limiting our conversations to those people who were immediately seated near us. After several preordered appetizers—interesting combinations of plant-based ingredients that were beautifully presented— our main entrees, also beautifully presented, were served. As dinner ended, we confirmed with Michael and Michel about their visit the next day and exchanged contact information before saying our goodbyes for what was a lovely dinner. As Michel was talking to Laëtitia, I asked them if I could take a photo—a wonderful memory of the evening.

On returning home, I looked up more information about Michel Auder. I learned that besides Warhol superstar Viva, he had been married to Cindy Sherman, the influential contemporary artist known for her self-portrait photography in made-up guises of stereotypical female roles, film noir scenes, and historic contexts. By strange coincidence, Joe and I had just taken a midterm for a contemporary art history course we were taking at Ohio State University and Cindy Sherman was one of the artist prompts on the test.

The next morning, I got up early to prepare the house for the impromptu tour. Since neither Michael nor Michel had ever been to the house before, I pulled out the display board of historic and pre-restoration photographs that I use for tours to give them a better understanding of the state of dilapidation of the property when we purchased it. "Wow, I had no idea this existed. How could a property like this fall into ruin?" Michael exclaimed. "It's fortunate that we discovered the house on such a beautiful day. We were so moved by the beauty and potential that we overlooked the amount of work and expense that lay ahead of us. Once you start a project like this there is no turning back!" I said with a laugh. "We spent almost every single day for about four years working on this project, but looking back, all the hard work was well worth it. You appreciate something you put so much effort into." Although both were artists, the fact that Michael fabricated pieces in both wood and metal had him discussing with Joe the technical aspects of the restoration. "Erin's father owns a timber framing business, so I have access to raw materials and equipment," Michael explained. "So that's how you fabricated those wonderful wood beams for the bench-like piece in the show?" I asked. "Exactly. I have a beautiful old timber-framed barn to work in as a studio as well."

As Joe pointed out details that a fellow craftsman would appreciate, I provided Michel with history, along with tales of the trials and tribulations of the project. "We didn't worry about designing spaces for resale value, but for our own lifestyle," I explained, showing them our open bedroom and bathroom space. "We wanted the views of the woods instead of a wall in our private space. Instead of dressers taking up space, we have only this floating platform bed with an adjoining room with a concealed wall of drawers and closets," I explained. "My ex-wife Cindy Sherman has a system like this.

It's perfect!" Michel responded, seeing the built-in cabinetry that conceals our wardrobe. After the house tour, Joe asked them if they would like to see the tower. "Absolutely!" they replied. I warned them it's a really rough construction site, but that was not an issue for them.

After the tower tour we walked them to their car. As we passed the garden, there were still Thai chili peppers hanging from the plants. "Do you mind if I take some for lunch?" Michael asked. "Help yourself!" "I will take some too," Michel added.

CHAPTER 24:
Instance No. 2:
EXPOSURE

W e got up early on Sunday, the day of the performance, and just as I finished making beds and doing some final wipe-downs, performers and Beeler staff started to arrive. I quickly urged Maren to get dressed, since our lack of window and door coverings means no privacy! We are shielded from neighbors and the outside world by thick vegetation, but when there are visitors wandering the site, only the Point Room bathroom has full privacy.

Soon the caterers, photographers, and others made for a festive atmosphere, and participants started setting up for the event. We were lucky to have perfect weather, with not a cloud in the sky, while the unusual heat of the last few days had passed. There was a slight autumn chill in the air, perfect for a light sweater, while a gentle breeze created a subtle movement of the trees. Laëtitia, although she was busy orchestrating the numerous activities, took the time to make sure how I felt about this invasion of so many souls, asking, "Are you okay with all of this?" "I've been through this before with tours," I replied. "I'm excited to see what you have created for the space!" Her warm smile and calm demeanor suggested that I would soon find out.

Just then, Ian arrived with JiaHao, one of the gallery assistants, carrying a large wooden object that turned out to be the bar he had fabricated for our bedroom. The structure was to rest on the raised concrete plinth that was the step up to our bathtub. Used to handling artwork, his deft maneuvering inside the tight entrance went smoothly, and soon the piece was secured in its position. Ian had measured as well as taken photographs on Monday during dinner, so the piece fit perfectly without a chance of tipping. Bartenders and servers dressed in black pants and crisp white shirts from Brothers Drake Meadery arrived, carrying bags of ice, bottles of spirts, and several cartons of the Vier5 *EXPOSURE* cocktail glasses. "This must be weird to see your bedroom suite turned into a bar!" Ian joked. "It's definitely a first!" I laughed, as the noisy ice crashed into the tub.

Maren came up to me and asked if I wanted her to build a fire in the firepit. After the heat of the past few days, no one had even considered the option. "That sounds like a good idea with the chill in the air. I'll ask Laëtitia what she thinks, it might be too smoky with the breeze, though." I thought it would be a great job for Maren, displaced from her usual bedroom habitat, and unfamiliar with the art crowd that was descending on her home.

I found Laëtitia trying to decide the best location for the caterer to set up the food tables. Initially, the white-linen-covered tables were set up adjacent to the flat boulder on the edge of the landscape arc, but Alana, the caterer from Harriet Gardens, thought that the seat height wall of canal stones would provide a better set up for replacement trays. Laëtitia asked me what I thought. "It doesn't matter to me. You might want to consider the sunlight. The canal stones are more in shadow in the afternoon from the tall spruce trees." Settled. Shade was beneficial for the food while the vertical rock formation provided a nice backdrop to the horizontal table.

"I don't want to interfere with your plans," I said to Laëtitia, "but Maren suggested that it might be nice to light a fire in the outdoor firepit. I'm sure she will be glad to attend to the fire during the event so you wouldn't need to find someone to maintain it." "That's a wonderful idea!" she replied. We walked over to the area just beyond the western bedroom, past a young Asian student with shoulder-length hair practicing Tai Chi, over to where six knee-height irregular boulders formed a circle about eight feet in diameter. "This is like a surrealistic dream," I said to Laëtitia as we passed the young man. "Just wait! We have a performer who drove all the way from Tennessee who will be performing down by the creek," she told me with a smile and sparkle in her eye. As we reached the firepit, I commented, "It's far enough from the house that it won't interfere. My only concern would be whether the smoke might interfere with the performers outside?" I asked. "I love the idea! Maren will not mind?" replied Laëtitia. "Not at all. She takes pride in building perfect fires." With that decided, Laëtitia turned and said, "Let's go in and get the first drink!"

Our bedroom was bustling with people setting up for the event. The bartender, a young African American woman with pulled-back hair and a crisp white shirt, stood on the raised platform next to the tub, in front of the waist-high, linen-draped bar that Ian and JiaHao had built. The top of the bar was arranged with rows of *EXPOSURE* cocktail glasses along with a large bowl of fresh mint leaves. Laëtitia asked the woman to please prepare cocktails for us. She had collaborated with Ian's friend Dru, an artist who also worked at Brothers Drake Meadery, to develop a "cinematic cocktail made of love, addiction, and randomness." The cocktail was made from Peach Rush Mead, OYO White Rye, St. Germaine (an elderflower liquor from France), and cherry juice, with a "smash" of mint at the end. After mixing the drink, the bartender came to adding mint. Laëtitia demonstrated that after the cocktail was prepared, she wanted the mint to be smashed with a double clap into each cocktail as part of the ritual. We clinked our glasses together, toasting with a "salut" and taking a sip of the honey-based beverage that had just a hint of tartness, which helped take the edge off my nerves just prior to the event's start.

As we stood over the low platform bed that Joe had designed years before we met, I admired our colorful Marimekko Tikkula Spice duvet in reds, magenta, oranges, and lime green, which had been covered in recent months to protect it from the puppy. Folded at the end of the bed was a Target quilt, used for the pup protection, that reminded me of the iconic Gee's Bends quilts that I loved but could only admire in museums. Laëtitia was also staring at the cover. At first I thought she was admiring the vibrant pattern, but she asked me, "Would you mind if we covered the bed with this quilt?" I explained that the quilt was a cheap cover I used to protect the duvet from the pup, but I would be glad to spread it over the top if she liked. As I spread the chartreuse, goldenrod, cream, and brown quilt, Laëtitia commented, "No, I was thinking we turn it over to the solid side," referring to the textured cream color of the opposite side. "This will be the perfect place to display the Vier5 poster." She asked someone to stack the posters designed for the event on the bed so that attendees would walk into the room and be drawn in by their bold graphics.

Each Instance of *Season Two* had an accompanying poster that provided background and insight about the development of the program. After interviewing me about both the history of the house and our restoration, Danny Marcus, art historian and Lichtenstein Fellow at the Columbus Museum of Art, wrote the text that accompanied the day's experience. Adjacent to a bold graphics of *WATER* and *EXPOSURE* on the Vier5 poster for *Instance No. 2*, he wrote:

In the history of architecture, the element of water is most often treated like a zoo animal, charming to look at, but from a safe distance. Channeled into waterfalls and reflecting pools, water plays the part of architecture's foil, performing the beguilements of Nature—the Eternal Feminine—opposite hard dick culture. But the powers of water are not so easily constrained. Shrugging off the zookeeper's commands, water eats away at hard-set concrete, penetrating skylights and casements, disintegrating facades and spreading rot and ruin in its wake. Reluctant to confront water on equal footing, most architects opt for a pantomime of mastery, conjuring spurting fountains and supine ponds fit for Narcissus. In the end, however, water dominates: the ceiling drips, the pool leaks, and the forces of fluidity advance.

Laëtitia is a friend of water. Her work explores hidden currents and counterblows in the archives of modern art, architecture and design, focusing on the role of women architects and artists, non-Westerners, and vernacular makers both inside and along the margins of the avant-garde.

The poster provided a history of the property, from its conception by three young designers to the degradation of the structure from years of neglect after it was left abandoned.

Water gives and water takes. On the afternoon of Oct. 13, 2019, Badaut Haussmann invites visitors to engage the past and future of the Gunning House, conjuring its original occupants as well as the site's environmental forces and flows. As if temporarily suspending the forward motion of historical time, a team of dancers, Tai Chi practitioners and artists will animate the concatenated memories of the Gunning House (which Robert and Mary regarded as a person in its own right), its trio of designers, and the surrounding landscape.

Someone announced the arrival of the bus carrying the attendees. With limited parking on site, a bus was the only way to transport such a large number of people to the property. Laëtitia gave the performers a directive to get into place. Carrying our cocktails, we parted ways and went outside to greet the guests. We walked past a beautifully displayed table of cut vegetables, tiered plates filled with fruit and multiple bowls of hummus made from root vegetables in bright autumn colors, artistically prepared by Alana from Verdic Table. Jo-ey led the procession of approximately fifty people up the driveway from the road. Laëtitia spoke for a few minutes, introducing several people including us, then provided the guests with a history and welcomed them to fully explore the property.

Like so many noteworthy events in life, the hours flew by, leaving fragments of memories, some in great detail while others are just a fleeting image, smell, or recollection of the moment. I recall the wind rustling through the trees, causing the occasional spruce cone to come crashing to the ground with a thud. I remember the earthy smell of hickory wood burning in the firepit, sparks crackling as the smoke drifted into the air. I remember how surreal it was to see the place bustling with life amidst a backdrop of chatter, music, and autumn color. Servers in crisp black and white outfits carrying trays of cocktails conjured up visions of the soirees hosted by Rob and Mary Gunning in the distant past. The performers were positioned throughout the site, carrying out their roles to fulfill Laëtitia's vision. There was a woman grating oranges—a symbol of new beginnings and life—onto one of the flat, table-like boulders, which gave off a strong citrus aroma, while another performed a similar action in the zen garden. JiaHao had taken a position near the bonfire performing Tai Chi, the smoke slowly drifting through his skillful maneuvers. Down below in the ravine, the sun glistened through the trees as Eric, the performer from Tennessee, rested atop the russet leaves along the bank of the slowly moving creek. Those who ventured out to the former tennis court, now reclaimed by nature, found a secret bar set up beneath the shade of a tree growing through uplifted cracks in the old surface. Inside, groups of people attentively observed the rhythmic beats of a tap dancer's shoes as they struck the Masonite plate that Ian had placed as a dance stage, their sounds echoing throughout the house over layers of muffled conversation. In the living room, the television monitor displayed the text of Mary Gunning's heartfelt letter from 1941 to Tony Smith, as it was read aloud by a young woman. At the dining room table sat three women appearing to play a game, while aromatic lavender and oranges were scattered nearby.

Groups of people observed and chatted as they meandered from room to room and around the property. Our good friend Chris, who I knew from the preservation advocacy group, Citizens for a Better Skyline, came with his girlfriend, Suzie. He had visited many years ago with Ted van Fossen, one of the original designers, as well as during the restoration while the house was mostly deconstructed for repairs. Jane Murphy, the professor of architecture who initially contacted me about Laëtitia's search for a site, was there with artist friends, including Ann Hamilton, a celebrated visual artist who I had known initially as a customer in my store. Jo-ey had told me that Ann's son had visited Glenbrow during the period when it was abandoned and had written a paper on the site. I mentioned to Ann that if he was interested in touring the house when he was in town, we would be glad to oblige. Although we tried to remain in the background, we spoke with many people who had visited the house in its ruinous state, amazed at the transformation.

Before long, the bus arrived to transport the attendees back to Beeler Gallery. The hours had flown by. While the staff members dismantled the temporary set up, we asked if any remaining staff were interested in a tour of the tower. "It's still a construction site," I told Laëtitia and Jo-ey, who had toured the tower last winter, "but we've made some progress." Since the spring, Joe had removed the thick translucent plastic covering the broken glass and had installed new windows, which brought light into the spaces and provided a splendid view of the ravine. He had also added a horizontal row of fixed counter-level windows, nine inches tall and extending nearly ten feet in length, that had originally been incorrectly measured for use in the main house. The room was now much brighter than their previous visit. Sunlight filtered through the stained-glass squares, which cast colored patches on the plywood subfloor, while the tree canopy outside the windows gave the impression of being in a treehouse. We made our way up the winding stairs to the bedroom level. "I built this *brise soleil* not only to provide a filtered privacy, but as a way to install these large windows from the exterior," Joe explained. I pointed out, "This window here is an egress window required for bedrooms, but it also brings more light into the room from the opposite direction." "We added this translucent panel to provide light and privacy as well the addition of a biophilic element with the long green strands of grass," I added, pointing to the sea grass embedded resin. Joe described the intended positioning of the bed and the layout of the bathroom before we headed up to the roof terrace.

The late afternoon sun struck the golden leaves of autumn, which, coupled with a steady breeze, provided a picturesque setting for a toast to the day. As the group conversed, I went back to the house and grabbed a couple bottles of cold wine and glasses before returning to the tower's roof terrace. I asked Joe to open the first of the two, a bottle of Ruffino Orvieto. Ian commented that the vineyard was connected to members of his family back in Italy. "How perfect to use it to toast such a wonderful day!" I commented as we poured wine into the glasses. Glasses clinked as we saluted the memorable success of Laëtitia's *EXPOSURE*.

The months leading up to *Instance No. 2* were like a crescendo in a musical piece, full of activity and rising anticipation, but with the toast atop the tower, our lives returned to a sense of normalcy. After we attended a celebratory dinner that evening, we said our goodbyes to people who had become fixtures in our daily lives and went back to restoration. We had met many interesting people during the past months, connections that would never have happened without our house restoration. There were still several more Beeler Gallery Instances in *Season Two* in the upcoming months, so the friendships we had developed would continue.

Afterward, I got a chance to discuss the meaning with Laëtitia. She explained, "I like to think of an orange as another representation of how our world could go as compared to an apple and all that it represents in capitalism. An orange would be a kind of socialist—as a cure and as a collective fruit. In its natural form, this fruit is meant to be shared, and the shares are equal." She explained to me that using an apple in this context has 1980s symbolism—New York and now, of course, as the brand. "An orange is a collective thing. Also, its smell is an antidepressant, which is very important regarding the effects of capitalism on our psychic and emotional lives." Her explanation provided new meaning to the memorable day.

CHAPTER 25:
Continuation of Enrichment

The morning after the event, Joe resumed work on the tower, concentrating on the tedious finish work around the new windows that had recently been installed. With the two-person jobs complete, he decided to work alone, so Adam left to work on other jobs. After the large transformation of the window installation, trim work, with its measuring, cutting, nailing, priming, and painting is time-consuming by comparison. Still, once the work is complete, the visual progress is significant and noticeable as things move closer to completion.

I resumed work on the rear gabion wall, entailing further trips to the stone yard, with the work of carefully packing the rocks in tight arrangements as I filled the cages with a mixture of varying stone types and colors—all with rounded edges. I had run out of flat, rounded stone from the creek, so the second cage that contained all newly purchased rocks appeared noticeably brighter than the first. After I finished the second basket, I summoned Joe to wire the lid onto the top. "I think you need to find more stone from the creek so there isn't such a difference," he suggested. "You need to add more of the weathered rock from the creek and mix them." I agreed, although that meant more trips down to the creek, venturing further downstream in search of similarly weathered, disc-shaped stones. As each cage of mixed patinated and new stone was completed, Joe secured the cages with their lids. The weight and mass of the stone would invariably deform the wire cages, so securing the tops with wire meant leaning against the stone planter while using both feet to push the gabions back into shape while Joe secured the lids.

On a Sunday afternoon in November, Michael Stickrod, the artist we had recently met during Beeler Gallery opening, was hosting an open house community tea along with his wife, Erin, at the Denison University Art Space in nearby Newark, Ohio. Maren had recently been asking about Newark after receiving a book about Louis Sullivan, a Chicago architect famous for both his beautiful organic motifs and for being acknowledged as the "father of the skyscraper." Sullivan was also well-known as "Leibermeister" to his best known protégé—Frank Lloyd Wright. Late in his career, he designed a number of small-town, midwestern banks, known collectively as the "Jewel Box Banks," one of which was The Home Building Association Bank in Newark, Ohio. The Sunday of the afternoon tea had clear skies, so it was the perfect opportunity for Maren to join us and photograph the building, as well as many other historic structures nearby.

We left a little early so we could take advantage of optimum sunlight. I had never been to Newark, knowing only that it was adjacent to Granville, the home of Denison University and the site of many cross-country meets during the kids' middle and high school years. Expecting to see a small downtown with boarded-up windows, I was pleasantly surprised by the well-maintained old buildings lining the courthouse square.

The focus of the square was the majestic 1878 Second Empire Style Licking County Courthouse, constructed of limestone and featuring a grand clock tower at its center. The deep blue sky provided the perfect backdrop for the gleaming white exterior, glowing in the bright sunlight. Unfortunately, the building we had come to view, the Louis Sullivan "Jewel Box," was shrouded in scaffolding while undergoing a total exterior restoration. We were still able to catch glimpses of the colorful mosaic-tiled facade and intricate organic terra-cotta ornamentation.

Michael Stickrod and his wife, Erin Kirwin, hosted several events at the Denison Art Space during their four-month art residency with Denison

University, which featured an installation called "The Hive"—a joint project that incorporated natural materials from the surrounding landscape of Licking County. The gallery space was located in a storefront of an old brick building that was just around the corner from the square and featured an impressively long elbow-height tea bar that Michael had fabricated from local ash wood. Behind the bar, shelves contained their collection of mismatched cups and mugs that they had amassed over the years, along with a lower shelf of kettles holding specially brewed teas. The teas Erin offered were made from locally sourced ingredients that she had collected from their farm. I selected a tea made from pine needles and apples—perfect after the chilly photo shoot.

In the front window of the storefront housing the art space was a large piece of sculpture that Michael had created from the massive root of a tree extracted from the ground, parts of which extended out like tentacles to hold aprons, jackets, and other work-related items. A yellow workplace safety light illuminated the piece. Several other pieces featured beeswax, including one formed into a coiled snake with an embedded wick—flickering with its glowing flame. Before leaving, we exchanged information so that we could have them over for dinner after Michael's upcoming Beeler event.

During November, two more Instances occurred, which featured a screening of Michel Auder's *May '68 in '78* (subtitled footage Auder filmed in 1978 that was recently edited by Michael Stickrod) in which he filmed Parisians' many personal reflections on the tumultuous period of civil unrest in Paris during 1968. The footage had been lost and was only recently recovered. After months of editing, the film was publicly premiered within the gallery space that was configured with several benches and cots for attendees.

Laëtitia also returned in November along with filmmaker Julia Trotta to present *Forget to Be Afraid: A Portrait of Linda Nochlin*. Julia was the granddaughter of Linda Nochlin, the pioneering feminist art historian well known for her 1971 article "Why Have There Been No Great Women Artists?" Joe and I had read this article as an assignment for the contemporary art history class we were taking at Ohio State University, so the timing was most opportune. Julia's close relationship with the iconic Nochlin provided an intimate conversation about an issue that still needs to be more fully addressed today.

November is blustery, cold, and gray—a prelude to the winter yet to come. Animals go into hibernation and insects go dormant while the remaining foliage drops from tree branches. The northern winds blow the dried leaves into piles around the edges of the open landscape. On the rare occasion that the clouds part and we get a rare glimpse of the bright giant orb in the sky, we take the opportunity to clean up the gardens, with one last mowing of the lawn to mulch the remaining leaves. Cooler temperatures allow for thicker clothes, which provide protection from thorny bramble as we descend the hillside, clippers in hand, to remove the last vestiges of summer undergrowth and vines. The banks of the creek become littered with several inches of russet-colored leaves. Those that drop into the creek accumulate around the protruding rock clusters.

Although bare trees extend your vista, the property seems smaller as the neighboring houses across the ravine come into view through the skeletal branches. Through the boughs of the spruce grove and denuded dawn redwoods, the neighboring subdivision can also be seen. The once verdant hillside fades to brown as the plants retreat in anticipation of winter.

Once Thanksgiving arrives, the entire holiday season seems to fly by. We have adopted a minimalist approach to decorating, far different from when Maren and Fia were children. Gone are the days of ten-foot Fraser firs that would take three days for Joe to meticulously arrange in alternating rows of warm and cool twinkling LED lights, followed by boxes and boxes of ornaments, all sentimental, gathered over the years. Collections of nutcrackers, strings of colored lights, strands of bunting, and countless ornaments have all been relegated to storage bins in the studio— consigned for use in the kids' future homes. Glenbrow's low seven-foot ceilings and limited space are not conductive to tall trees and opulent decorations. Instead, a single five-foot vintage aluminum tree is placed in front of the corner window, decorated with colorful orbs in oranges, magenta, chartreuse, and yellow—unbreakable in case of pup attacks. Pine bunting and a single wreath decorate the front of the house. "You're like a grinch!" my family complains, always eager to decorate, but noticeably unavailable when it's time to take it all down and pack everything away. "Ever hear of 'less is more?'" I asked them.

Beeler Gallery held a screening of Michel Auder's 1970 film, *Cleopatra,* his decadent reinterpretation of the 1963 blockbuster film starring Elizabeth Taylor and Richard Burton. The cast featured Warhol Factory regulars that included Auder's wife, Viva, as Cleopatra. The film's surrealistic portrayal of the Queen of the Nile was destroyed by its disgruntled producer and never shown to the public. This would be its premiere screening, close to fifty years later!

CHAPTER 26:
Landscape

The new year, 2020, arrived without much fanfare. Warmer than usual temperatures brought cold rains and only minimal dustings of snow. The dread of the snowplows' repeated driveway deposits of grimy slush that would later freeze never materialized the entire winter. In fact, this was the first winter that we never had to shovel at all—very strange for central Ohio. Still, without heat in the tower, work progress there was at a standstill.

The warmer weather, however, did not minimize the doldrums of winter. With extra time on our hands until spring, when work could resume, we decided to take a landscape architecture course at Ohio State University. The class kept us busy going to campus twice a week, joining in the mass of individuals searching for a parking space, then having to maneuver around various campus construction projects, all while enjoying many architectural gems on our way to class.

By weird coincidence, the lecture portion of the class was held in Ramseyer Hall, a 1932 beaux arts-style building on the Ohio State University's massive campus that once housed the experimental high school attended by Ted van Fossen when he first met Rob and Mary Gunning. It was Ted who, impressed with the enchanting landscape, chose the site for Glenbrow and later would help design many components of the project.

Tuesdays meant recitation after class, held at Knowlton Hall, the elegant modernist building clad in marble shingles designed by Mack Scogin and Merril Elam, which houses the Knowlton School of Architecture. Our younger daughter, Sofia, was finishing up her final year there, so we often had requests to deliver goods to her. "I have another all-nighter coming up so can you bring me snacks and fruit?" she would request. She popped in right before class started, and she often asked Joe for a design critique on her project, filled us in on the latest intrigues of her close-knit group of friends, or offered details about the latest themed party they were planning at their house. "Do you have any Betsey Johnson outfits for me to borrow for our eighties party? What jewelry do you have to go with it?" she would ask, never thinking of not fully accessorizing an outfit. "Now that we're students, maybe we should come to your party?" I would joke, as a look of fear spread across her face!

Our course was a history of the American landscape, from the wilderness before European settlers arrived until the present, studying how the land has been shaped and reshaped to fit the ever-changing needs of the population as the young country grew. The course caused me to reflect on how the landscape around Glenbrow had changed drastically before and since that fortuitous trip that Ted van Fossen made with Rob and Mary Gunning in 1939.

The land in central Ohio has changed over time from the shallow seas and marshes of millions of years ago to the vast icy glaciers some tens of thousands of years ago that created the lakes, formed the river valleys, and deposited our rich, fertile soil. In later prehistoric times, the Adena Culture were early inhabitants of the land. Although mainly hunters and gatherers, they also domesticated a few native plants into food sources. They are often referred to as Mound Builders because they buried their dead in ceremonial mounds. As the size and complexity of these earthen forms increased, some of the indigenous people were subsequently referred to as the Hopewell Culture. They resided near waterways to support their agricultural development as well as to establish trade routes between their settlements from around 100 BCE to 500 CE. Most notably, they created the Great Circle Earthworks and Octagon Earthworks in nearby Newark, Ohio. These impressive wonders are spread across four square miles of area and their orientation was thought to have played a role in the ceremonial and astronomical rituals of their creators.

Later, several Native American nations lived in what later became the central Ohio region, peacefully trading with French traders until the mid-eighteenth century when American colonists pushed westward as they confiscated land inhabited by Native Americans. The Haudenosaunee Confederacy, commonly referred to as the Iroquois Confederacy, were made up of six Native American nations that were pushed west into Ohio by European settlers. By the 1770s, they had moved into central Ohio, integrating with members of the Miami and Shawnee nations. By 1831, the United States government forced the Ohio Seneca to sell their land and move onto reservations in present-day Oklahoma.

Glenbrow's site and the surrounding land were first surveyed in 1796 as part of the five-mile-square townships, deemed "Military Lands," that were allotted to veterans for their service in the army. It was after the survey that the land saw radical changes as it was cleared by homesteaders for crop and livestock husbandry.

The original 1.37-acre plot had originally been part of the Cady Farm since 1879, with small parcels sold off along Broad Street in the late 1920s and early 1930s, before it was finally purchased by Robert Gunning in 1940. The property included both flat, cleared land and the hillside down to the creek, with a small triangle of land at creek level that was excluded so that the Cady family animals could maintain access to the clear creek water from the east side of the ravine. The tiny plot was gifted to us in 2018 by James Cady. Farmland surrounded the Gunning plot at the time the house was first built. In Mary Gunning's January 31, 1941, letter to Tony Smith she describes:

The ravine and stream with ice—the trees with snow edging the dark branches and there across to the level of farmland. Young David Sweet and I watched two men loading corn shocks on a wagon one day last week. We watched until the men drove their team of horses off to the barn. Then we saw a red bird against the snow.

During a visit in September 2016, Ted van Fossen's only son, Tony van Fossen, now a professor in Australia, recounted how he and Tom Gunning used to collect Indian arrowheads along the banks of the creek and up along the hillside. While the flat land had been regularly tilled by farmers, the steep hillside had remained untouched for centuries.

In 1955, Rob Gunning purchased an additional 1.137 acres from the Cady family to allow for enough land to construct a tennis court. Broad Street at the time was still a rural, two-lane road with farmland surrounding their property. It would be years later that suburban sprawl would begin, accelerated by the 1972 opening of Mt. Carmel East Hospital and the 1975 completion of the eastern section of the I-270 outer belt that surrounds Columbus. It wasn't until the mid-1990s that the Cady family sold a large portion of their acreage to a developer and a suburban subdivision was built, including six tract homes that presently extend along the western boundary of the property behind the ruins of the tennis court.

CHAPTER 27:
Season Finale

The winter of 2020 also included several more Instances that we attended as part of Beeler Gallery's *Season Two*. Each event was a reunion of friends and offered exposure to cutting-edge art. During a dinner with Michael Stickrod and his wife, Erin, in December, we discussed how we would love to host a dinner after Michel Auder returned for the January 30 showing of *Subversive Historian*, a video in which Stickrod edited over 20,000 hours of footage from fifty years of work by Auder filmed in France, New York City, upstate New York, and rural Ohio, as a portrayal of his life.

The text that accompanies the piece, written by art historian and NYU professor Robert Slifkin, describes the film: "Using Auder's highly personal footage as raw material for his own loosely nimble editing—and equally adroit selection—Stickrod underscores Auder's restless commitment to chronicling realms of experience typically deemed unworthy of documentation and preservation, which, nonetheless, contains deep, unguarded knowledge of the past and, perhaps, even wisdom for the future." It was quite a visually impressive compilation that presents snippets of Auder's unconventional life—and those he interacted with in the past—as seen through both his own cinematography and that of his friend, Michael Stickrod.

The show also included *Staples and Rubber Bands, Sculpture and Video: 1969–2019*, featuring numerous works the two artists had created together and individually. Artist/educator Liz Roberts introduced the video presentation and the sculptural pieces before large screens set up in the small gallery filled with

Stickrod's dried goldenrod installation, as well as in the open gallery space near the skeletal bleachers from earlier exhibits, both spaces highlighted with Badaut Haussman's ethereal, shimmering drapes as a backdrop.

Joe and I rushed back to Glenbrow after the video presentation to set up for a dinner to honor the two celebrated artists. Although I had baked bread and prepared a vegetarian lasagna ahead of time, I knew they enjoyed spicy food as well. "I remember how you and Michel picked some hot peppers from my garden last fall, so I prepared a roasted poblano sauce for dinner," I told Michael.

We enjoy hosting informal large gatherings of such interesting people and using the island (peninsula—eyes roll!) seating for overflow when the dining room is full. Other artists, who were in town for the video debut and as part of *Instance No. 7* being held the following day, joined us for dinner along with Beeler staff. Heide Hinrichs, a Brussels-based German artist, attended the dinner along with Liz Roberts. After many bottles of wine, out came the grappa, so we were grateful for ride-sharing services for our guests. Nothing bonds people better than a good dinner, glasses of wine, and the ensuing conversations.

Heidi was joining Columbus artist Laura Larson in dialogue at Beeler Gallery the following day to discuss *Second Shelf,* the international effort to expand library collections on publications by nonbinary, female, and queer artists, and artists of color. Heidi also displayed over 100 of her drawings— reinterpretations of work by other artists included in the *Second Shelf* project that were displayed on strands of twine suspended from the high ceiling.

Beeler Gallery scheduled their final event, *Instance No. 8: An Art Book Affair,* on the evening of February 29 and afternoon of March 1, 2020. The events surrounding these two days included performances, exhibits, presentations, and live music, along with a bookfair hosting twenty-six exhibitors and publishers. I knew that this would be Laëtitia's final visit from Paris, so I contacted her to ask whether she would be interested in us hosting a final dinner for her with attendees of her choosing.

The first event of *Instance No. 8* was a performance piece jointly created by Laëtitia and Danny Marcus, the art historian who had interviewed me about the history of Glenbrow before writing the text for *Instance No. 2*. The latest piece, entitled *Water-Prelude*, was an extension of Badaut Haussmann's opening piece for *Season Two* entitled *WATER*. Both pieces included an homage to French architect/designer Charlotte Perriand, a historic figure who shared Badaut Haussmann's desire to seek a deep connection to a site before formalizing a concept. In *Water-Prelude*, dancers recreated memories from Perriand's autobiography that ended with her steamship voyage to Japan after the Nazi invasion of France during World War II. The rippled iridescent curtains that defined the blueprint of the Museum of Modern Art in Kamakura, Japan, also brought to mind the feeling of being surrounded by water, especially as the performers moved up and down with their backs against the walls, like the ebb and flow of tides or the motion of waves. The dancers interacted with the experimental music with muffled vocalizations as they moved through the galleries filled with bookfair participants. As the performers entered the dark screening room, guided only by the narrow beam of a flashlight, the silence allowed the spoken word to become discernible.

Water above and water below
Water that gives and water that takes
Water within and water between
Water before and water to come

We left early to prepare for Laëtitia's dinner to celebrate the success of *Season Two* and say our final goodbyes. Unfortunately, this meant we were going to miss several other works and workshops. Achim Reichert of the Paris Vier5 held a graphics workshop, working with CCAD students, on experimental typefaces. Artist and educator Suzanne Silver's *Dots for John, Dashes for Emily, Punctuation for Everyone* was a conceptual piece performed in the main gallery. Using large glass megaphones, shoe tapping, and unusual experimental sounds, excerpts from John Baldessari and Emily Dickinson were translated into morse code. Afterward, the No Wave band, Voidgig, performed in the main gallery. Gina Osterloh, Liz Roberts, and Melissa Vogley Woods formed the three-piece band that played conceptual counterculture music.

One of the positive aspects of hosting frequent dinner parties and giving tours is that you keep your house well-organized and clean to the point of having little preparation to do. Usually the island ("Actually, it's a peninsula," Joe would insistently correct me), with its location just inside the front entrance, is a magnet for clutter. "Where it lays is where it stays!" seems to be the kids' motto. Mail, receipts, hats, gloves, and water bottles would all collect under the assumption that the one who despised the mess the most (as in *moi!*) would find the proper place for each deposited item. Having events planned ensures that things are put away before chaos can reign. Also, while entertaining, the landscape is similarly well kept, with the grass always mowed and the gardens weeded in warm weather, and walks are shoveled clear when it snows. Keeping the house maintained for an event also prohibits Joe from starting new projects that mean he will leave tools and supplies strewn around his work area. Normally, winter is a time for interior projects, but this winter, we had an active event schedule that included regular entertaining.

After arriving back at Glenbrow to prepare for the evening, I baked bread, prepared appetizer plates, and made a salad with greens, fennel, and pomegranate seeds, while Joe made several batches of fresh pasta. I made two sauces, one a kale pesto sauce and the other tomato-based with assorted roasted vegetables. Knowing that more people than usual were coming, I also made a vegetarian couscous dish. Once the bread was in the oven, I cut up fresh berries to serve with an assortment of cookies for dessert. I made sure there was an ample supply of wine to toast the success of *Season Two* and to bid farewell to our newfound friends of the last several months.

It was a festive night with much to celebrate. The nearly five months of programming had enriched the lives of those who attended, as well as creating many new friendships. As soon as our guests each had a glass of wine in hand, I provided tours to those who had never been to the house before, while Joe was left to refill glasses and play solo host in my absence. We reminisced over the events of the past several months. There were invitations to visit many faraway places and we reminded our friends that they were likewise welcome to visit us as well. As it did during the *EXPOSURE* performance of last October, time seemed to fly by as we said our goodbyes to people who had become part of our lives, made possible through the good fortune of restoring the property.

CHAPTER 28:
Everything Changed

P reoccupied by daily life at Glenbrow, our class assignments, and art events, we were in a forward trajectory without much attentiveness to the world outside our bubble. After the March 1 celebratory dinner, that all changed in a blink of an eye. Just as spring was reemerging, our lives were awakened from the idyllic slumber we had known since moving into Glenbrow. The sense of focus on our restoration projects and the enchanting landscape that had so encompassed daily life abruptly shifted from our peaceful surroundings to the chaotic world of the pandemic. Within two weeks from entertaining guests, we were in strict quarantine.

We were fortunate to be in such a bucolic setting to be sequestered. Springtime at Glenbrow is sublime, witnessing the rebirth as nature comes back from dormancy, regardless of all the upheaval occurring in the outside world. The quarantine brought a calm, as the hustle and bustle of the workweek virtually ended overnight. Traffic and airplane noises greatly diminished, enhancing the audibility of songbirds, mating frogs, cicadas, and crickets. Without the usual outside pressures of daily life, we were afforded a time for reflection.

When we drove through the opening in the tree line past the dangling vines on that warm September afternoon in 2013, we had no idea the casual detour would lead to such an enrichment of our lives. What was it about this property, in its obvious state of advanced ruin, that moved us to change our course? Why not build a new home on our Bexley lot, or even less risky, find an existing house that suited our needs without an avalanche of unknown costs and the commitment of time?

The splendid landscape gave us such a sense of repose. Even our children felt an immediate attraction to the beauty of the setting. The three original young visionary designers interpreted the principles of organic architecture that had inspired them while working with the great master, Frank Lloyd Wright. The open meadow and wooded ravine provided an ideal landscape to build a home that would complement the natural setting—Rob and Mary's house "could be designed to marry the open field with the wooded ravine," Ted van Fossen later wrote. They used natural materials such as old growth cypress, nicely weathered to blend into the landscape, and staggered courses of rough-hewn stone, quarried on site. Siting the house low to the ground so it appeared to grow out of the landscape as it snaked along the edge of the ravine, the house offered a captivating view of the woods and stream, while providing a comforting sense of shelter and privacy from the many intrusions of the busy road.

Inside, instead of typical rooms, the open and continuous floor plan provides space that flows freely, while the generous windows and doors along the ravine ensure that nature is an integral part of daily life. Natural colors, the warmth and texture of the wood-grain plywood panels, and the playful hidden figures you find embedded in the surface of the stone enrich your sensory experiences as the light and shadows of the sun and moon move across the floor. The scale of the house is designed to be in proportion to the human figure. The primordial notion of prospect and refuge satisfies basic human instincts. This was a home that was designed to inspire and enrich the lives of the people who would inhabit it.

We were not the first to be drawn in by the enchantment of the property, despite its ruinous state, but we had the experience, fortitude, and financial means to take on a restoration of this complexity. Once you delve into a project of this scale, there is no turning back. You just bite the bullet and forge ahead. Architectural restoration, even with hands-on experience, is not for the faint of heart.

Years of sacrifice, hard work, and financial worry have paid off beyond our wildest expectations. The experiences we encountered, the interesting people we have met, as well as the delight of living every day in such a sublime environment, close to nature, are well worth the sacrifice of time and money. In her 1941 letter to Tony Smith, Mary Gunning expressed the sentiment perfectly: "I never get through with the joy of looking and there is always a quiet and a peace and yet a deep excitement."

AFTERWORD

A year of quarantine at Glenbrow afforded me time for reflection, freeing me of many distractions of daily life. What started out as documentation of the history I uncovered and the process untaken of our restoration for my daughters and future owners, turned into this public narrative. It was my correspondence with our good friend, Nora Sojourner Chalfont-eldest daughter of Rob and Mary Gunning, that convinced me to share our experiences with others.

I want to thank the Gunning family for sharing their historic documents and wonderful memories of growing up at Glenbrow. I am also grateful to their parents, Rob and Mary Gunning, for their willingness to take a risk on on three talented young designers: Tony Smith, Ted van Fossen and Larry Cuneo, over 80 years ago.

I also want to thank the Tony Smith estate, especially Sarah Auld, who provided me with archived correspondences, historic photographs and background material. Their comprehensive website, tonysmithestate dot com is a wealth of information on the life and legacy of this accomplished artist and renaissance man. I hope the future holds publication of Tony Smith's 1943 unpublished manifesto, "The Pattern of Organic Life in America", where my opening Smith quotation originated.

I also want to thank contributors to the 1998 Museum of Modern Art exhibition catalogue, *Tony Smith: Architect, Painter Sculptor*, Robert Storr, John Keenen and Joan Pachner whose compendious research and insightful reflections provided me with a better understanding of Tony Smith.

I also would like the folks at Parafine Press, publisher Anne Trubek, editor Michael Jauchen and their staff in helping make *Red Bird Against the Snow* a reality.

Lastly, I want to express my most sincere gratitude and deep love to my family. My daughters, Maren and Sofia Kuspan who assisted me in photography and editing, and especially to my husband, Joe Kuspan, whose vision, expertise and detailed editing of the technical process involved in recording the restoration of Glenbrow, made this book possible.

NOTES

EPIGRAPH

Tony Smith, "The Pattern of Organic Life in America," unpublished manuscript, 1943. Courtesy of the Tony Smith Estate.

CHAPTER 1

City of Woodstock, Illinois: https://www.woodstockil.gov/community/page/woodstock-celebrity-status.

CHAPTER 2

Sheban, Jeffrey. "1940 Home Influenced by Wright in Danger," *Columbus Dispatch*, December 6, 2008. https://www.dispatch.com/article/20081206/LIFESTYLE/312069688.

CHAPTER 5

History on Tony Smith: Storr, Robert, John Keenan, and Joan Pachner. "Tony Smith: Architect, Painter, Sculptor," Museum of Modern Art, New York catalog, 1998.

Chronological timeline of Tony Smith: http://www.tonysmithestate.com/about/chronology.

Ted van Fossen's account of finding the Blacklick site: Mary Gunning eulogy by Ted van Fossen, delivered August 17, 1986.

Tony Smith design philosophy: Historic papers from Columbus Landmarks Foundation.

Theodore van Fossen (Rush Creek Village, OH) home in danger Dec 6, 2008, started by David C., Wrightchat, The Frank Lloyd Wright Building Conservancy discussion forum.

Information on Tony Smith's wife, Jane Lawrence: Smith, Roberta. "Jane Lawrence Smith, 90, Actress Associated With 1950's Art Scene, Dies." *New York Times*, August 22, 2005. https://www.nytimes.

com/2005/08/22/arts/design/jane-lawrence-smith-90-actress-associated-with-1950s-art-scene.html.

Information on Ted van Fossen's wife, Maggie Belgrano: https://www.legacy.com/obituaries/newspress/obituary.aspx?n=margaret-belgrano-de-mille&pid=173872533.

Correspondence between the Gunnings and Tony Smith: Archives of Tony Smith Estate.

Details about Ted van Fossen at Glenbrow: Interviews with Nora Chalfont Gunning.

Robert Gunning's funeral: Canterbury, William. "Rob Gunning's Last Party," *Akron Beacon Journal*, July 13, 1980.

CHAPTER 6

Santer, Rikki. "The Readability of Place; Blacklick, Ohio," https://columbuslandmarks.org/wp-content/uploads/2014/01/December_2013-Cornerstone.pdf.

Information on the Cultural Landscape Foundation: https://tclf.org/landslides/gunning-house-columbus-oh-risk.

Thomas Gunning background: https://arthistory.uchicago.edu/faculty/profiles/gunning.

CHAPTER 7

Quotes on Glenbrow from Wrightchat: http://www.wrightchat.savewright.org/viewtopic.php?f=2&t=3095&hilit=Gunning.

CHAPTER 14

Letter from Mary Gunning to Tony Smith courtesy of the Tony Smith Estate.

CHAPTER 18

Information on Laëtitia Badaut Haussmann: https://thecreativeindependent.com/people/visual-artist-laetitia-badaut-haussmann-on-maintaining-focus/.

https://www.arteporexcelencias.com/en/news/labbel-artistic-laboratory-
  bel-group.
Background on Jo-ey Tang: https://www.ccad.edu/blogs/curator-and-
  artist-jo-ey-tang-lead-ccads-beeler-gallery.

CHAPTER 19

MoMA Organic Design competition: https://assets.moma.org/documents/
  moma_catalogue_1803_300190105.pdf.
History of Eames chair: https://eames.com/en/lcw.

CHAPTER 21

Beeler Gallery *Season Two: Follow the Mud*, curated by Jo-ey Tang,
  co-curated by Ian Ruffino and Marla Roddy, 2019–2020. https://www.
  beelergallery.org/season-two-follow-the-mud/.

CHAPTER 22

Text from *WATER* and *EXPOSURE* written by Daniel Marcus, art
  historian and Lichtenstein fellow at Columbus Museum of Art.

CHAPTER 24

Symbolism behind *EXPOSURE*: Personal correspondences with Laëtitia
  Badaut Haussmann and Jo-ey Tang.

CHAPTER 25

Hildebrand, Grant. *The Wright Space: Pattern and Meaning in Frank
  Lloyd Wright's Houses*, Seattle: University of Washington Press, 1991.

CHAPTER 26

Information on Ohio Native Americans: http://ohiohistorycentral.org/w/
  Hopewell_Culture
https://ohiohistorycentral.org/w/Seneca-Cayuga_Indians.

CHAPTER 27

Background on Michel Auder and Michael Stickrod's *Subversive Historian*: https://beelergallery.org/instance-no-6/.

Information on *Instance No. 8* performances: https://beelergallery.org/artbookaffair2020/.

Symbolism behind *Instance No. 8* performance piece: Correspondence with Danny Marcus.

CPSIA information can be obtained
at www.ICGtesting.com
Printed in the USA
LVHW080548240721
693464LV00007B/94

9 781950 843466